TRUMP

TRUMP

A GRAPHIC BIOGRAPHY

TED RALL

NEW YORK / OAKLAND

ACKNOWLEDGMENTS

Elise Capron, Sandy Dijkstra, Jon Gilbert, Lauren Hooker, Bonnie D. Miller, Dan Simon

■   ■   ■

A Seven Stories Press First Edition

Seven Stories Press
140 Watts Street
New York, NY 10013
www.sevenstories.com

Library of Congress Cataloging-in-Publication Data

Names: Rall, Ted, author, cartoonist.
Title: Trump : a graphic biography / by Ted Rall.
Description: New York : Seven Stories Press, 2016.
Identifiers: LCCN 2016024563 (print) | LCCN 2016024694 (ebook) | ISBN
   9781609807580 (pbk.) | ISBN 9781609807597 (E-book)
Subjects: LCSH: Trump, Donald, 1946---Comic books, strips, etc. | Trump, Donald,
1946---Juvenile literature. | Presidential candidates--United States--Biography--Comic
books, strips, etc. | Presidential candidates--United States--Biography--Juvenile literature.
| United States--Politics and government--2009---Comic books, strips, etc. | United
States--Politics and government--2009---Juvenile literature. | Presidents--United States-
-Election--2016--Comic books, strips, etc. | Presidents--United States--Election--2016--
Juvenile literature. | Graphic novels.
Classification: LCC E901.1.T78 R35 2016 (print) | LCC E901.1.T78 (ebook) |
   DDC 333.33092 [B] --dc23
LC record available at https://lccn.loc.gov/2016024563

Printed in the USA.

9 8 7 6 5 4 3 2 1

TRUMP

ONCE UPON A TIME, THE UNITED STATES OF AMERICA RULED THE WORLD.

IN MANY WAYS, WE STILL DO.

FOR A LONG TIME, HOWEVER, ORDINARY AMERICANS HAVE FELT THAT THEY WERE WORKING HARDER. EARNING LESS. PAYING MORE.

WE WORK HARD. BUT WE CAN'T GET AHEAD. INSTEAD, WE'RE FALLING BEHIND.

WE'VE BEEN IN DECLINE FOR 40 YEARS. BUT WE
AMERICANS ARE OPTIMISTS. SO WE'VE KEPT
OUR HEADS DOWN, STRUGGLED TO GET BY,
AND WAITED IN VAIN FOR THINGS TO TURN
AROUND. ALL OVER THE COUNTRY, FACTORIES
HAVE CLOSED, JOBS OUTSOURCED OVERSEAS.
CITIES HAVE BEEN HOLLOWED OUT. HOPELESS
AND HELPLESS, TOO MANY PEOPLE HAVE
TURNED TO HEROIN AND METH.

THE EROSION OF THE MIDDLE CLASS IS A STORY MOST AMERICANS STRUGGLE WITH EVERY DAY. BUT IT RARELY APPEARS ON TV. AND IT'S ALMOST NEVER A POLITICAL ISSUE.

LGBT "BATH-ROOM" LAW

EVICTION

IF A PROBLEM ISN'T ACKNOWLEDGED, THERE'S NO CHANCE THE POLITICAL CLASSES WILL TRY TO FIX IT. THE MIDDLE-CLASS SQUEEZE HITS MINORITIES HARDEST, OF COURSE. BUT FOR WHITES, DOWNWARD MOBILITY IS NEW.

WE CAN'T PAY FOR YOUR COLLEGE **AND** YOUR MOM'S OPERATION.

WORKING- AND MIDDLE-CLASS WHITES ARE
TAKING THEIR LOSS OF ECONOMIC WELL-
BEING HARD. THEIR PARENTS DID BETTER THAN
THEIR GRANDPARENTS, YET THEY'RE DOING
WORSE THAN THEIR PARENTS. AND THEIR KIDS
ARE IN EVEN BIGGER TROUBLE. THIS IS A RICH
COUNTRY. BUT WORKERS ARE NOT SHARING
IN THE AMERICAN DREAM. SOMEONE MUST BE
TO BLAME.

IN A COUNTRY THAT WILL SOON BE LESS
THAN HALF-WHITE, SOME WHITES SAY THE
PROBLEM IS IMMIGRATION.

Press "1"
for English

THIS
IS
AMERICA.
WHY DO
I HAVE
TO DO
THAT?

WTF?

"Disney forced
workers to
train their
Indian
replacements
before firing
them."

THE MIDDLE CLASS WAS ALREADY ON THE ROPES. THEN, IN 2007, THINGS WENT FROM BAD TO WORSE.

THE HOUSING BUBBLE BURST. WALL STREET SPECULATORS CRATERED THE MARKET FOR SUBPRIME MORTGAGE DERIVATIVES, ERASING BILLIONS OF DOLLARS IN STOCK AND REAL ESTATE VALUE IN MONTHS. BANKS FAILED. MILLIONS LOST THEIR JOBS. FAMILIES PLUNGED INTO POVERTY AND "INVISIBLE HOMELESSNESS": CRASHING ON THEIR FRIENDS' AND RELATIVES' COUCHES...NOT-SO-TEMPORARILY.

CAPITALISM ITSELF WAS ON THE ROPES.

AS BUSH PREPARED TO TURN THE WHITE HOUSE
OVER TO OBAMA IN LATE 2008, OFFICIALS
OF BOTH ADMINISTRATIONS WERE TOLD THE
ECONOMY WOULD TANK UNLESS THEY SAVED
BANKS THAT WERE "TOO BIG TO FAIL." DAYS,
EVEN HOURS, MATTERED. PANICKED POLITICOS
SCRAMBLED TO RESPOND.

WHAT TO DO?

OPTION I WAS A "RETAIL" APPROACH: THE
FEDERAL GOVERNMENT COULD BAIL OUT THE
MILLIONS OF HOMEOWNERS FACING EVICTION
DUE TO PLUNGING PROPERTY VALUES OR JOB
LOSS. THIS WOULD KEEP THESE PEOPLE IN
THEIR HOMES, WHICH WOULD SHORE UP THE
MORTGAGES UNDERLYING THE TROUBLED
SECURITIES, WHICH WOULD IN TURN SAVE THE
BANKS. THIS APPROACH WOULD PREVENT
FURTHER PROPERTY DEVALUATION CAUSED BY
THE BLIGHT THAT FOLLOWS EVICTIONS.

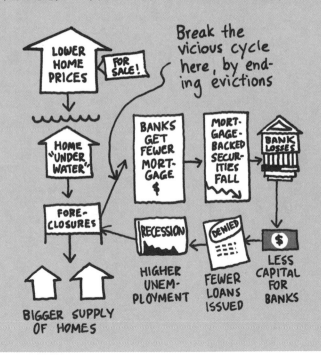

BUT OPTION I WAS POLITICALLY FRAUGHT.

OFFICIALS AND THE MEDIA WORRIED ABOUT "MORAL HAZARD" -- ENCOURAGING BAD BEHAVIOR BY FAILING TO PUNISH IT.

WHAT ABOUT HOMEOWNERS WHO SIGNED ON TO LOANS THEY COULDN'T AFFORD IN THE FIRST PLACE? SHOULD THEY BE BAILED OUT...?... THE ANSWER, SOME SAY, IS AN EMPHATIC **NO**.

Eric Weiner, Reporter

BAILING OUT MAIN STREET WOULD BE COMPLICATED. NEW BUREAUCRATIC INFRASTRUCTURE WOULD BE REQUIRED.

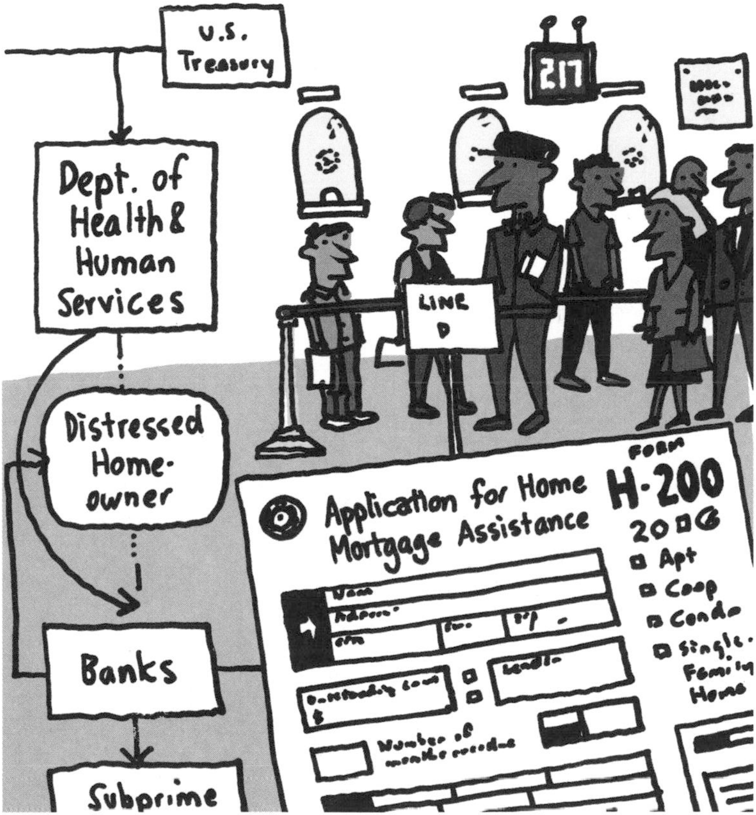
U.S. Treasury
Dept. of Health & Human Services
Distressed Home-owner
Banks
Subprime
217
LINE D
FORM H-200
Application for Home Mortgage Assistance
Apt
Coop
Condo
Single-Family Home

SO BUSH AND OBAMA'S ECONOMIC TEAMS
CHOSE OPTION 2: THE "WHOLESALE," DIRECT
BAILOUT OF THE INVESTMENT BANKS, NO
STRINGS ATTACHED. BAILING OUT WALL
STREET WAS STRAIGHTFORWARD AND QUICK.

SINCE WALL STREET WAS CONNECTED TO
BOTH WHITE HOUSES, EVERYONE INVOLVED
ALREADY KNEW ONE ANOTHER. HANDSHAKE
DEALS WITH A FEW DOZEN BANKERS AND THE
DEAL WAS DONE. BY MARCH 2009, THE FED
HAD MADE A WHOPPING $7.77 TRILLION
AVAILABLE TO THE BANKS UNDER THE
TROUBLED ASSET RELIEF PROGRAM (TARP).

FOR THE BANKS, THE TARP BAILOUT WORKED SPLENDIDLY. IN NO TIME, PROFITS WERE SOARING. CEO SALARIES HIT NEW RECORDS.

THE RECOVERY WAS UNDERWAY, ECONOMISTS DECLARED.

EVERYONE WAS HAPPY.

WELL, NOT EVERYONE.

CITIZENS HARMED BY THE HOUSING CRASH
RECEIVED LITTLE TO NO HELP. THE BANKS HAD
PROMISED TO LOOSEN CREDIT, BUT WITH NO
LEGAL REQUIREMENT FOR THEM TO DO SO,
THEY SAT TIGHT. SO BUSINESSES COULDN'T
EXPAND. JOBS REMAINED SCARCE.
FORECLOSURES AND EVICTIONS CONTINUED.
SPECULATORS, RICHER THAN EVER, SNATCHED
UP FORECLOSED HOMES AT BARGAIN PRICES.

AMERICANS SEETHED. IT WAS SO UNFAIR. SOME
VENTED THEIR OUTRAGE VIA STREET POLITICS.
ON THE LEFT, ANGRY PEOPLE JOINED THE
OCCUPY WALL STREET MOVEMENT. ON THE
RIGHT, ECONOMIC POPULISM FOUND ITS HOME
IN THE TEA PARTY.

ILLEGAL IMMIGRANTS FROM MEXICO, TEA PARTIERS BELIEVED, WERE STEALING THEIR JOBS AND DRIVING DOWN WAGES. IT WAS TIME TO PUT AMERICANS FIRST. TEA PARTIERS WANTED LAW-BREAKING FOREIGNERS KICKED OUT AND THE BORDERS GUARDED SO LAW-ABIDING AMERICANS COULD FIND WORK AGAIN.

DON'T TREAD ON ME

Senator Ted Cruz speaking at a Tea Party rally during 2015 government shutdown

WITHIN A FEW YEARS, HOWEVER, THE GRASSROOTS POPULISM OF THE TEA PARTY HAD BEEN DEFANGED, CO-OPTED BY BIG DONORS LIKE DICK ARMEY AND THE KOCH BROTHERS, AND BROUGHT INTO THE REPUBLICAN PARTY FOLD.

BUT NATIVISTS DIDN'T GO AWAY. FIGURES LIKE "AMERICA'S TOUGHEST SHERIFF," JOE ARPAIO -- KNOWN FOR TENT PRISON CAMPS IN THE ARIZONA DESERT WHERE PRISONERS ARE ABUSED, HUMILIATED, AND SOMETIMES KILLED -- BECAME RIGHT-WING HEROES.

OPPOSITION TO IMMIGRATION BECAME SO NORMALIZED THAT PRESIDENT OBAMA, A DEMOCRAT, FELT COMPELLED TO ORDER A RECORD NUMBER OF DEPORTATIONS. BUT NATIVIST REPUBLICANS SAW OBAMA'S ACTIONS AS TOO LITTLE, TOO LATE. THEY WERE STILL RESTIVE. BUT THEY HAD NO OUTLET WITHIN ELECTORAL POLITICS.

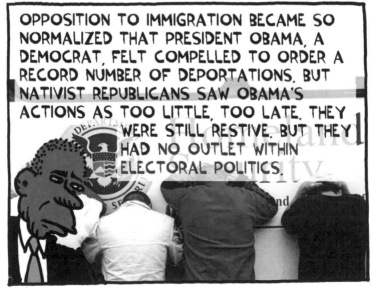

ILLEGAL IMMIGRATION HADN'T BEEN A MAJOR
ISSUE IN THE 2012 ELECTION. AS AMERICANS
GEARED UP FOR THE 2016 PRESIDENTIAL
CAMPAIGN, IT APPEARED THAT IT WOULD BE
IGNORED AGAIN.

THIS WAS SUPPOSED TO BE ONE OF THE MOST
BORING ELECTIONS IN MEMORY, BETWEEN TWO
DYNASTIC RETREADS: FORMER FIRST LADY/
SENATOR/SECRETARY OF STATE HILLARY
CLINTON, DEMOCRAT, VERSUS PRESIDENT'S SON/
PRESIDENT'S BROTHER/FORMER FLORIDA
GOVERNOR "JEB" BUSH, REPUBLICAN.

 politics

Election Results   2016   Natic

Sear

2016: A Bush-Clinton rematch?

By Gloria Borger, Kevin Bohn and Brian Rokus, CNN
Updated 7:40 PM ET, Thu April 24, 2014

Clinton v Bush: America is getting the
dynastic matchup it said it didn't want

Hillary Clinton

America deserves better than Clinton v Bush

It looks like 2016 will be a Bush v Clinton rematch. But the primaries are full
of angry alternatives representing different ideological responses to the same
problem - the impoverishment of American ideals

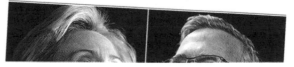

BEFORE THE 2016 CAMPAIGN BEGAN (IN SUMMER 2015), A WHOPPING 86% OF REPUBLICANS TOLD POLLSTERS THEIR MOST IMPORTANT ISSUE WAS THE ECONOMY, MORE IMPORTANT THAN TERRORISM OR FOREIGN AFFAIRS.

TAXES SHOULD BE LOWER, SIMPLER, FAIR AND CLEAR.

Jeb Bush

IF YOU ...THINK YOU OUGHT TO POUND THE RICH INTO SUB- MISSION, I GUESS YOU WON'T LIKE THE PLAN.

John Kasich

THE MAJOR GOP CONTENDERS PIMPED THEIR USUAL REAGAN-ERA SOLUTION: "TRICKLE- DOWN" ECONOMICS. CUT TAXES FOR THE RICH AND BUSINESS. HOPEFULLY, THEY'LL USE THE SAVINGS TO INVEST. WHICH WILL CREATE JOBS.

TRICKLE-DOWN NEVER WORKED. MOST PEOPLE KNEW THAT.

NATIVISM HAS ALWAYS BEEN A PART OF THE POLITICS OF POPULISM, LEFT AND RIGHT.

TRUMP TOOK AMERICA FIRSTISM FURTHER THAN ANYONE ELSE. HE DIDN'T THINK IMMIGRATION WAS ONE ISSUE AMONG MANY. HE SAW IT AS THE ISSUE OF THE CAMPAIGN.

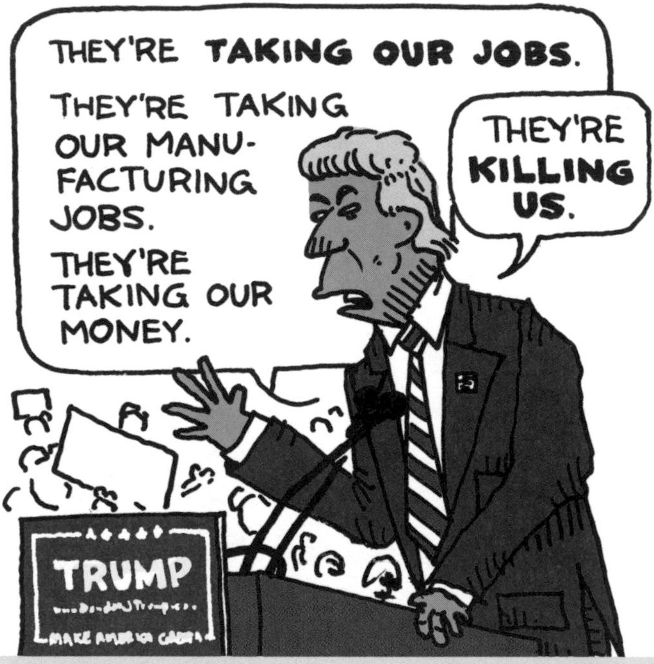
THEY'RE **TAKING OUR JOBS.**
THEY'RE TAKING OUR MANU-FACTURING JOBS.
THEY'RE TAKING OUR MONEY.
THEY'RE **KILLING US.**
TRUMP
MAKE AMERICA GREAT AGAIN

HE INTUITED THAT IT COULD FORM THE BASIS FOR A POLITICAL MOVEMENT. TRUMP SAID HE WAS RUNNING FOR PRESIDENT, WITH STOPPING ILLEGAL IMMIGRATION BY ANY MEANS NECESSARY HIS #1 ISSUE.

DONALD TRUMP WAS ONE OF 18 REPUBLICAN CANDIDATES FOR PRESIDENT. ALL OF A SUDDEN HE SHOT TO THE TOP OF THE HEAP. THEN HE STAYED THERE, STUNNING THE POLITICAL WORLD. WHAT WAS HIS SECRET? LIKE ANY GOOD BUSINESSMAN, TRUMP EXPLOITED AN INEFFICIENCY IN THE MARKETPLACE, IN THIS CASE, OF IDEAS.

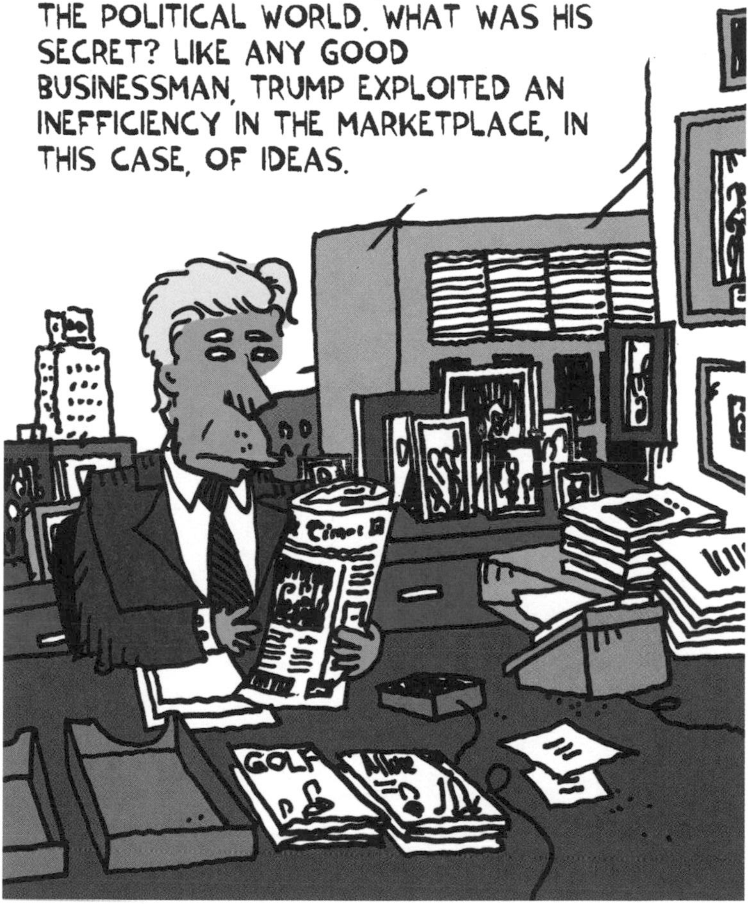
GOLF

HIS MARKET WAS READY-MADE. FOR YEARS, CONSERVATIVES HAD PLAYED THE POPULIST CARD, LAYING THE GROUNDWORK WITH THE ELECTORATE FOR A MOVEMENT COMPOSED OF THE THIRD OF VOTERS WHO THOUGHT THAT THEY WERE GETTING SCREWED BY UNDOCUMENTED WORKERS.

A COUNTRY THAT LOSES CONTROL OF ITS BORDERS

IS **NOT** A COUNTRY!

Pat Buchanan, Ex-Nixon staffer and Crossfire TV pundit August 12, 1995

MAINSTREAM REPUBLICAN POLITICIANS BASHED IMMIGRANTS. BUT THEY WERE NEVER GOING TO ACT. TOO MUCH OF THEIR PARTY'S MONEY CAME FROM BIG BUSINESS. CORPORATE BOARDS LOVED OPEN BORDERS, WHICH PROVIDED CHEAP LABOR THAT PUSHED DOWN EVERYONE'S SALARIES. TRUMP, ON THE OTHER HAND, WAS A POLITICAL OUTSIDER. HE CARED ABOUT HIMSELF. HE DIDN'T GIVE A DAMN ABOUT THE PARTY OR ITS BIG DONORS. HE COULD GO FURTHER THAN ESTABLISHMENT REPUBLICAN CANDIDATES.

HE COULD SHOCK. HE COULD OFFEND. HE COULD GET THAT THIRD OF THE VOTE.

IN *MEIN KAMPF*, NAZI LEADER ADOLF HITLER CALLED FOR GERMANY TO EXPAND EAST INTO THE SOVIET UNION (HIS *LEBENSRAUM* POLICY), ARGUING THAT HIS COUNTRYMEN NEEDED MORE SPACE. THE FORCED REMOVAL OF RUSSIANS, UKRAINIANS, AND OTHERS LIVING IN THE USSR WAS AN IMPLICIT PART OF HITLER'S PLAN.

HE WASN'T ALONE. DURING THE 1930s AND 1940s JOSEPH STALIN SUBJECTED POLES, KURDS, AND MANY OTHER ETHNIC POPULATIONS TO MASS REMOVAL TO REMOTE CORNERS OF THE SOVIET UNION. HISTORY JUDGES THESE AMONG THE 20TH CENTURY'S WORST CRIMES.

IN THE FALL OF 2015, DONALD TRUMP PLEDGED TO DEPORT ALL ESTIMATED 11.3 MILLION PEOPLE LIVING WITHOUT PAPERS IN THE UNITED STATES -- INCLUDING MILLIONS OF CHILDREN WHO HAVE NO MEMORY OF THEIR COUNTRIES OF ORIGIN -- "BACK WHERE THEY CAME [FROM]."

NEXT, TRUMP ADDRESSED ANOTHER ISSUE: THE THREAT OF ISLAMIC TERRORISM. EARLIER THAT YEAR, JIHADISTS INSPIRED BY THE ISLAMIC STATE OF IRAQ AND SYRIA (ISIS) HAD SLAUGHTERED A BUNCH OF CARTOONISTS AT THE OFFICE OF A SATIRICAL NEWSPAPER IN PARIS.

THIS IS AN ATTACK ON ALL OF HUMANITY AND THE UNIVERSAL VALUES WE SHARE.

IN NOVEMBER, THERE WAS A BIGGER ATTACK IN PARIS, DURING A ROCK CONCERT...

...AND LATER IN SAN BERNARDINO.

IT WAS HORRIBLE, BUT WHAT COULD ANYONE DO? GOVERNMENTS OFFERED THE USUAL LAME ASSURANCES THAT THEY WERE PURSUING LEADS. THEY LOOKED IMPOTENT AND CLUELESS.

TRUMP STEPPED FORWARD, BOLDLY PROCLAIMING THAT HE COULD KEEP AMERICANS SAFE FROM THE CARNAGE ABROAD.

AS WITH IMMIGRATION, HIS PRESCRIPTION FOR HOMELAND SECURITY WENT FURTHER THAN ANYONE ELSE'S.

IT WAS EXTREME. UNDER TRUMP'S PLANS, EVEN U.S. CITIZENS LIVING ABROAD WOULDN'T BE ALLOWED TO COME HOME.

AND A LOT OF REPUBLICANS LOVED IT.

IT TOOK A WHILE FOR THE PUNDITOCRACY
TO CATCH ON THAT EVERYTHING ABOUT THE
NEW PRESIDENTIAL CANDIDATE -- HIS
BELLIGERENT STYLE, HIS BIZARRE HAIR, HIS
TAKE ON REPUBLICANISM -- WAS POPULAR
PRECISELY BECAUSE IT WAS SO UNORTHODOX.

FOR EXAMPLE,
TRUMP WAS
ASKED IF HE
WOULD REQUIRE
MUSLIM
AMERICANS TO
REGISTER
THEMSELVES IN
A NATIONAL
DATABASE.

[I] would certainly implement that -- absolutely.

TRUMP EVEN SAID HE AGREED WITH FDR'S
DECISION TO SEND JAPANESE AMERICANS TO
CONCENTRATION CAMPS DURING WORLD WAR II.

POLITICS NOV 20 2015, 9:27 AM ET
**Donald Trump's Plan for a Muslim
Database Draws Comparison to Nazi
Germany**

POLITICS DONALD TRUMP

**Exclusive: Donald Trump Says He Might
Have Supported Japanese Internment**

THE FURTHER HE WENT, THE MORE APPLAUSE
HE GOT. HE DOUBLED DOWN.

DEMONIZING PEOPLE BASED ON THEIR RELIGION.
FORCED REGISTRATIONS AND DEPORTATIONS.
NAZIS DID THIS SORT OF THING. WAS TRUMP
SERIOUS? JOURNALISTS ASKED HIM. OVER AND
OVER, IN PERSON AND ON HIS ACTIVE TWITTER
FEED, HE SAID HE WAS.

REPUBLICANS WEREN'T DISGUSTED BY HIS
ANTICS. THEY APPROVED! IN AN 18-WAY
RACE, TRUMP SHOT TO THE TOP OF THE
POLLS IN THE GOP PRIMARY CONTEST,
QUICKLY TOPPING 30%.

IT IS TRUE THAT ILLEGAL IMMIGRATION
REDUCES WAGES FOR U.S. CITIZENS WITHOUT
A HIGH SCHOOL DIPLOMA.

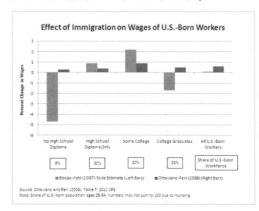

Effect of Immigration on Wages of U.S.-Born Workers

Source: Ottaviano and Peri (2008), Table 7, 2011 CPS.
Note: Share of U.S.-born population ages 25-64, numbers may not sum to 100 due to rounding.

IT'S A REAL PROBLEM, ONE THAT HASN'T
BEEN TAKEN SERIOUSLY BY LIBERALS OR
PROGRESSIVES. TERRORISM IS ALSO A
REAL THREAT, AS WE SAW ON 9/11.

THE TROUBLE IS, IT'S HARD TO SEPARATE
THE ECONOMIC NATIVISTS AND PEOPLE
UNDERSTANDABLY CONCERNED ABOUT
TERRORIST ATTACKS FROM THE CRAZIES
ON THE FAR RIGHT: RACIST SKINHEADS,
MILITIA TYPES, NEO-NAZIS, AND OTHERS
WHO ARE USUALLY, AND RIGHTLY,
MARGINALIZED FROM THE POLITICAL
PROCESS.

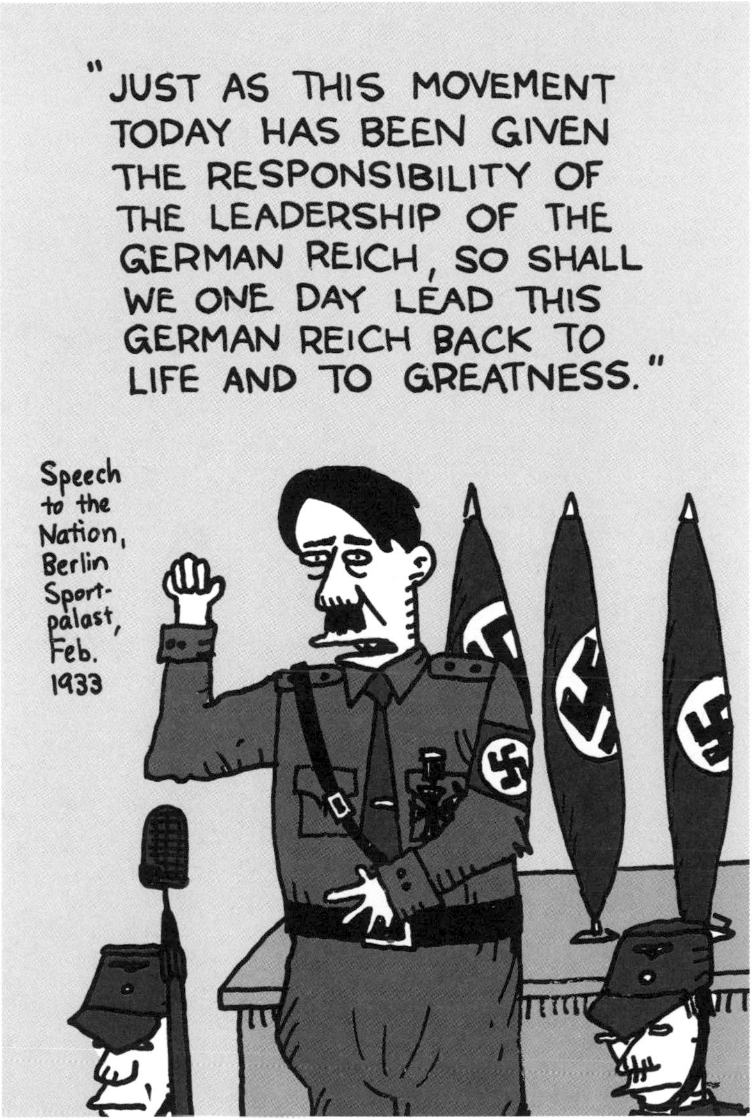
"JUST AS THIS MOVEMENT TODAY HAS BEEN GIVEN THE RESPONSIBILITY OF THE LEADERSHIP OF THE GERMAN REICH, SO SHALL WE ONE DAY LEAD THIS GERMAN REICH BACK TO LIFE AND TO GREATNESS."
Speech to the Nation, Berlin Sportpalast, Feb. 1933

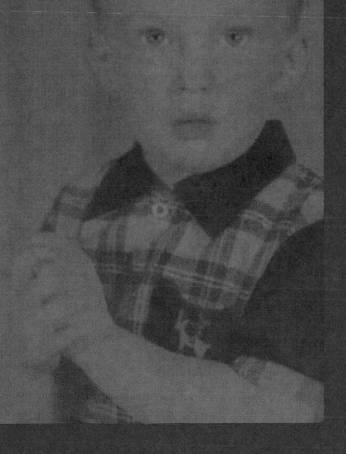

DADDY'S BOY

DONALD JOHN TRUMP WAS BORN ON JUNE 14, 1946, AT THE BEGINNING OF THE GREAT BOOM THAT FOLLOWED THE U.S. VICTORY IN WORLD WAR II. TRUMP WAS BORN INTO VAST WEALTH, THE FOURTH OF FIVE CHILDREN LIVING IN A BEAUTIFUL MANSION IN JAMAICA ESTATES, A LILY-WHITE ENCLAVE ON THE QUEENS SIDE OF THE NEW YORK CITY/LONG ISLAND BORDER.

DONALD JOHN'S MOTHER, MARY ANNE MacLEOD, WAS A STAY-AT-HOME MOM WHO'D BEEN BORN IN THE TINY VILLAGE OF TONG ON THE ISLAND OF LEWIS IN SCOTLAND.

HIS FATHER, FREDERICK CHRIST TRUMP (1905-1999), FOUNDED ONE OF THE BIGGEST REAL ESTATE EMPIRES NEW YORK HAS EVER SEEN.

THE SELF-MADE FATHER WAS AUSTERE AND HARD-WORKING, SETTING A HIGH BAR FOR INTEGRITY AND ACHIEVEMENT. IN ONE STORY, FRED FAMOUSLY SCOURED HIS CONSTRUCTION SITES AT THE END OF THE DAY FOR DISCARDED NAILS SO THEY COULD BE REUSED.

FRED ROSE ABOVE HIS PEERS IN A VICIOUSLY
COMPETITIVE BUSINESS. HE EXPECTED HIS SONS
TO DO EVEN BETTER THAN HE HAD. BUT HOW
WAS THAT POSSIBLE? *THE NEW YORK TIMES*
WROTE THAT FRED,

"like Sam LeFrak, another master builder, helped change the face of Brooklyn and Queens with thousands of homes for the middle class in plain but sturdy brick rental towers, clustered together in immaculately groomed parks. Although overshadowed in the news for the last two decades by his flamboyant son Donald, Mr. Trump, a self-made man, built more than 27,000 apartments and row houses in the neighborhoods of Coney Island, Bensonhurst, Sheepshead Bay, Flatbush, and Brighton Beach in Brooklyn and Flushing and Jamaica Estates in Queens."

DESPITE HIS SUCCESS, FRED WASN'T ABOVE
FIBBING. THOUGH BORN IN NEW YORK TO
GERMAN PARENTS, HE TOLD HIS JEWISH
TENANTS HIS FAMILY WAS SWEDISH.

OF THE FIVE TRUMP CHILDREN, ONLY DONALD AND HIS BROTHER ROBERT WOULD GO INTO THE FAMILY BUSINESS -- THE LATTER ONLY FOR A SHORT TIME. EARLY ON, HOWEVER, THE HEIR WAS FAR FROM APPARENT.

AS A YOUNG BOY, DONNY TRUMP WAS ENERGETIC, FEISTY, AND PETULANT -- A SPOILED AND DIFFICULT CHILD.

EXASPERATED, HIS PARENTS SENT HIM TO THE KEW-FOREST SCHOOL, IN THE FOREST HILLS SECTION OF QUEENS. HE WAS ALWAYS GETTING INTO TROUBLE. IN SECOND GRADE, HE EVEN PUNCHED A TEACHER BECAUSE HE THOUGHT SHE DIDN'T KNOW ENOUGH ABOUT MUSIC.

HEAD OF SCHOOL

WE USED TO REFER TO OUR DETENTION AS A **"DT"**— A "DONNY TRUMP"— BECAUSE HE GOT MORE OF THEM THAN MOST OTHER PEOPLE IN THE CLASS.

Paul Onish, one of Trump's classmates

PRESAGING HIS BAD-BOY ADULT PERSONA, TRUMP'S MISBEHAVIOR AND DISOBEDIENCE WAS SO OUTRAGEOUS THAT KEW-FOREST KICKED HIM OUT AT THE END OF SEVENTH GRADE. EVEN THE FACT THAT HIS INFLUENTIAL DAD WAS ON THE SCHOOL'S BOARD COULDN'T SAVE HIM.

SO DONNY WAS BUNDLED OFF TO THE NEW YORK
MILITARY ACADEMY, A PRIVATE BOARDING SCHOOL
UPSTATE IN CORNWALL-ON-HUDSON. IT WAS A BIG
CHANGE FOR THE RICH KID FROM QUEENS. CADETS
AWOKE AT DAWN, LEAPT INTO THEIR UNIFORMS
AND MARCHED IN FORMATION TO THE MESS HALL.

FIRST-YEAR CADETS ATE "SQUARED-OFF" -- THEY
LOWERED THEIR FORKS INTO THE FOOD AT A
RIGHT-ANGLE PATH AND, DEPOSITED IT INTO THEIR
MOUTHS IN THE SAME WAY.

THEN THEY RAN BACK TO THEIR DORMS
FOR INSPECTION.

AS HIS PARENTS HAD HOPED, DISCIPLINE SUITED 13-YEAR-OLD DONNY. HE DID A PERFECT JOB CLEANING THE RIFLES IN HIS CHARGE. HIS UNIFORM WAS IMPECCABLE. AT INSPECTION TIME, HE MADE SURE HIS BARRACKS WERE SPOTLESS.

DONALD SEEMED TO WELCOME BEING IN A PLACE WITH CLEAR-CUT PARAMETERS, A PLACE WHERE HE COULD FOCUS ON... HOW TO COME OUT ON TOP AND GET WHAT HE WANTED.

COCKSURE, POSITIVE... ANYTHING YOU CAN DO I CAN DO BETTER.

Gwenda Blair, Trump biographer

MIKE KABEALO, TRUMP'S ROOMMATE

THE TRUMP WE KNOW TODAY CAME TOGETHER AT NYMA. THAT'S WHEN HE DECIDED TO GO INTO REAL ESTATE, TO JOIN AND TAKE OVER HIS FATHER'S COMPANY. HE GREW TALL, AND EVEN MORE SELF-CONFIDENT. GIRLS WERE A PRIORITY.

Ladies' Man: TRUMP

THEN AS NOW, DONALD OBSESSED OVER HIS HAIR, COMBING IT OVER AND OVER. HE GREW HIS TRESSES AS LONG AS THE RULES ALLOWED.

FOR MOST PEOPLE, THE TEEN YEARS ARE ABOUT TRYING TO FIND YOURSELF. NOT FOR DONALD TRUMP. BY THE TIME HE WAS 15, TRUMP KNEW WHO HE WAS AND WHERE HE WAS GOING. GIVEN THAT HE COULD COUNT ON HIS FATHER TO BANKROLL HIM, HE WOULD ALMOST CERTAINLY BE ABLE TO ACHIEVE MOST IF NOT ALL OF HIS DREAMS.

THAT GAVE HIM TREMENDOUS CONFIDENCE, WHICH HIS CLASSMATES FOUND IRRITATING.

"[The way he laughed] made you feel like he was separating himself from you. It made you feel like there was an air of superiority. Just enough of a signal that he was laughing at you." —George White, Trump's classmate

TRUMP WAS COCKY. ON THE OTHER HAND, HE WORKED HARD -- ESPECIALLY IN ANYTHING REQUIRING COMPETITION. HE WASN'T A SPORTSMAN. HIS CUTTHROAT ATTITUDE GARNERED RESENTMENT.

I DON'T THINK HE HAD A HANDFUL OF LOYALISTS, YOU KNOW? BECAUSE HE WAS SO COMPETITIVE THAT EVERYBODY WHO COULD COME CLOSE TO HIM HE HAD TO **DESTROY**.

Ted Levine, Trump's roommate

DURING VISITS HOME, FRED AGREED TO
GROOM DONALD TO JOIN THE FAMILY
BUSINESS. HE ENROLLED AS A FRESHMAN AT
FORDHAM UNIVERSITY IN THE BRONX AND
SPENT WEEKENDS AT HIS FATHER'S SIDE.
AFTER TWO YEARS, HE TRANSFERRED TO THE
UNIVERSITY OF PENNSYLVANIA. THE TRUMPS
LIKED PENN BECAUSE IT HAD A
CONCENTRATION IN REAL ESTATE.

DONALD MAJORED IN ECONOMICS AT THE
WHARTON SCHOOL OF FINANCE'S
UNDERGRADUATE PROGRAM (NOT THE
FAMOUS MBA TRACK).

I WENT TO THE
WHARTON SCHOOL
OF FINANCE. I'M,
LIKE, A REALLY
SMART PERSON.

July 11,
2015

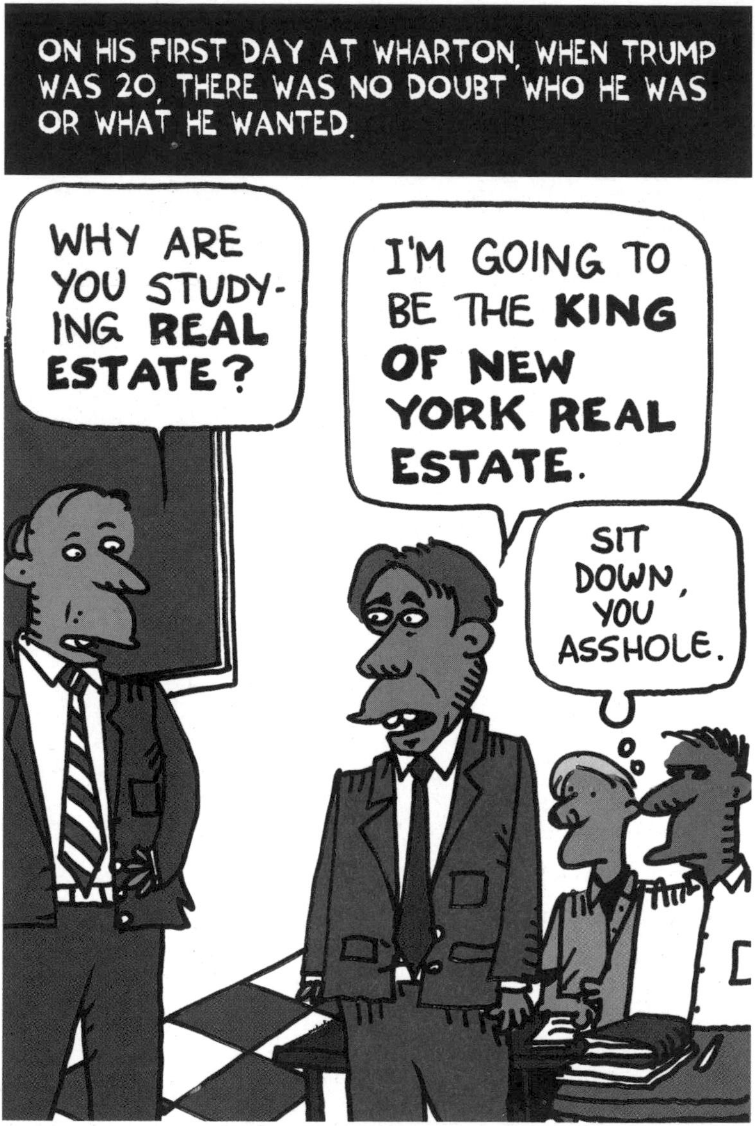
ON HIS FIRST DAY AT WHARTON, WHEN TRUMP WAS 20, THERE WAS NO DOUBT WHO HE WAS OR WHAT HE WANTED.
WHY ARE YOU STUDYING **REAL ESTATE?**
I'M GOING TO BE THE **KING OF NEW YORK REAL ESTATE.**
SIT DOWN, YOU ASSHOLE.

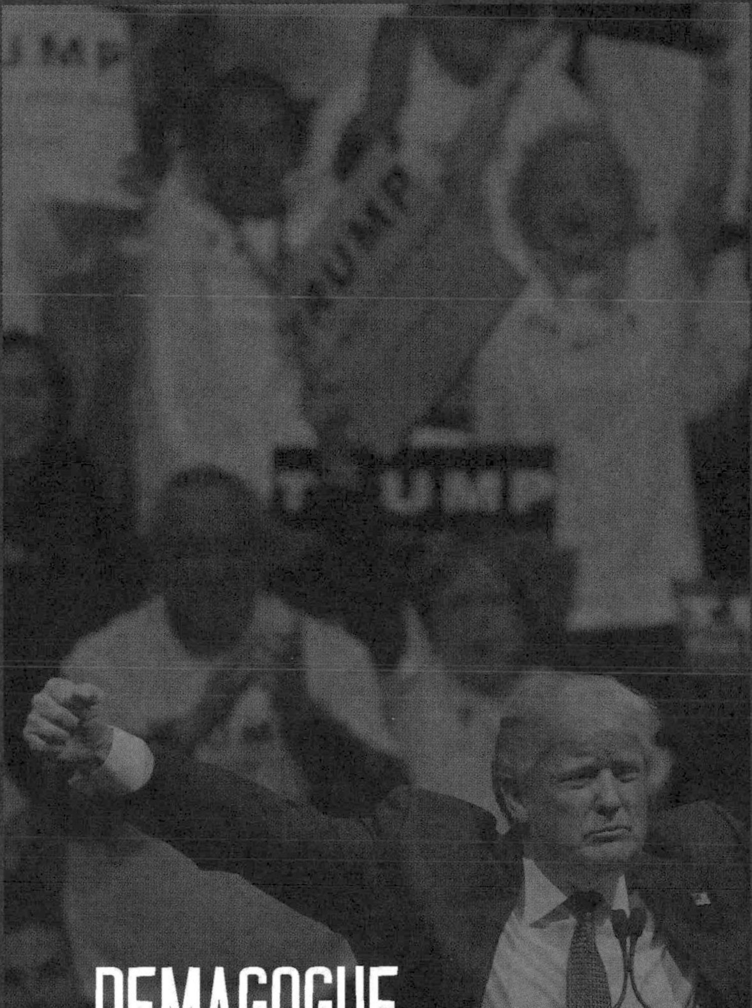

DEMAGOGUE

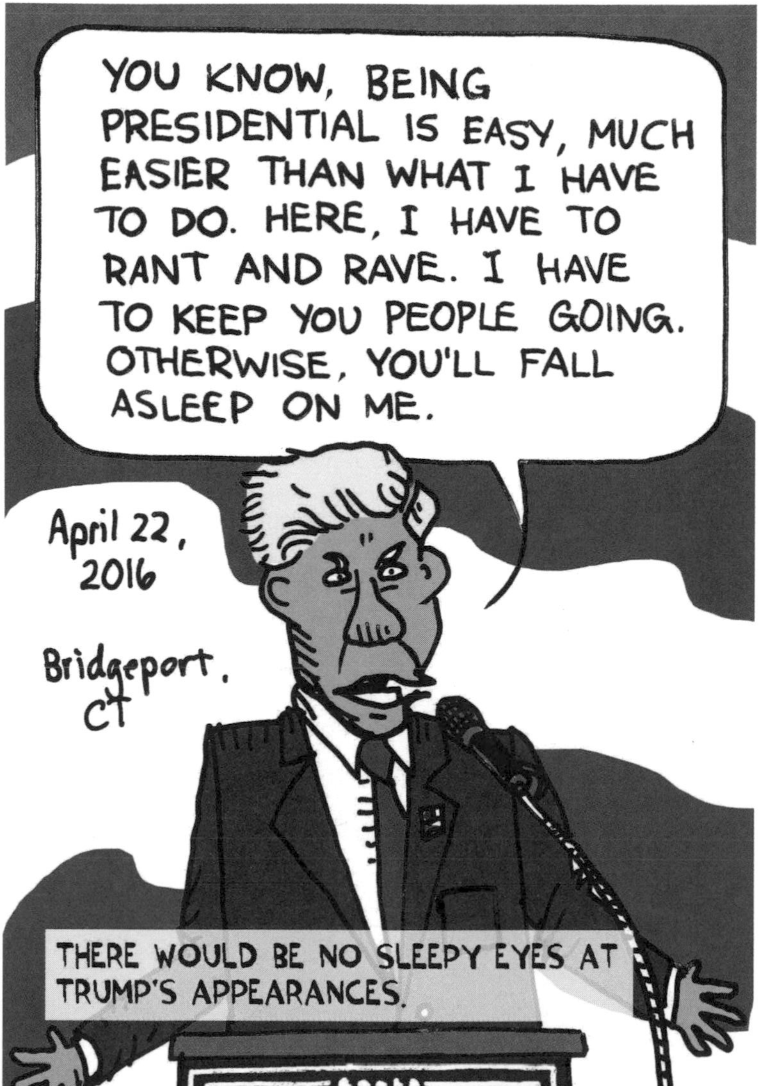
YOU KNOW, BEING PRESIDENTIAL IS EASY, MUCH EASIER THAN WHAT I HAVE TO DO. HERE, I HAVE TO RANT AND RAVE. I HAVE TO KEEP YOU PEOPLE GOING. OTHERWISE, YOU'LL FALL ASLEEP ON ME.
April 22, 2016
Bridgeport, CT
THERE WOULD BE NO SLEEPY EYES AT TRUMP'S APPEARANCES.

TRUMP'S RALLIES WERE WILDLY ENTERTAINING. THEY WERE ALSO SCARY. THE CANDIDATE'S SWEEPING, VAGUE PRONOUNCEMENTS AND VIOLENT TONE WERE REMINISCENT OF HITLER'S RALLIES AT NUREMBERG, MINUS THE AWESOME CHOREOGRAPHY. PROTESTERS AND A JOURNALIST WERE BEATEN UP.

I'D LIKE TO PUNCH HIM IN THE FACE, I TELL YA!

and, in Vermont:

CONFISCATE THEIR COATS. IT'S ABOUT -10° OUTSIDE.

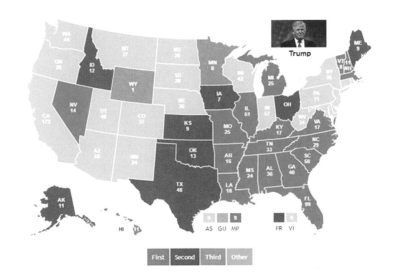

Trump

First | Second | Third | Other

OUTSIDE THE HUGE RALLIES, THERE WAS A CAMPAIGN TO RUN. BECAUSE TRUMP'S TEAM WAS A SKELETON CREW WHO DIDN'T BOTHER TO RESEARCH THE ARCANA REQUIRED TO COMPETE SUCCESSFULLY IN A CAUCUS STATE, TRUMP LOST IOWA, THE FIRST CONTEST IN THE NATION, TO TEXAS SENATOR TED CRUZ.

BUT HE QUICKLY RECOVERED AND WON NEW HAMPSHIRE AND SOUTH CAROLINA, THE FIRST KEY PRIMARIES (WHICH ARE MORE STRAIGHTFORWARD TO ENTER). STATE AFTER STATE, TRUMP KEPT WINNING.

"LOSERS." THE WORD EMBODIED TRUMP'S MANICHAEAN WORLDVIEW. AMERICA'S GOVERNMENT, HE CHARGED IN HIS ANNOUNCEMENT SPEECH, WAS RUN BY IDIOTS AND LOSERS.

> WE HAVE LOSERS, WE HAVE PEOPLE WHO DON'T HAVE IT. WE HAVE PEOPLE THAT ARE MORALLY **CORRUPT**. WE HAVE PEOPLE WHO ARE SELLING THIS COUNTRY **DOWN THE DRAIN**.

IF YOUR JOB HAD BEEN SHIPPED OVERSEAS BECAUSE OF NAFTA -- IF YOU'D LOST YOUR HOME IN AN ILLEGAL BANK FORECLOSURE FOR WHICH NO ONE WAS EVER PROSECUTED -- IF YOUR SON HAD LOST HIS LEG IN IRAQ -- WHAT COULD YOU DO BUT CHEER?

> "PATRIOTISM, PRESERVING AND PROTECTING THE UNIQUE CHARACTER OF OUR NATION AND PEOPLE, ECONOMIC NATIONAL-ISM, AMERICA FIRST, STAYING OUT OF OTHER NATIONS' WARS..."
>
> ~ Pat Buchanan defines what's behind Trumpism

TRUMP'S SUPPORTERS LOVED HIM. BUT THEY CAUGHT FLAK FROM THEIR FRIENDS. WHEN THEY HEARD THEMSELVES DESCRIBED AS FASCIST OR RACIST, THEY DIDN'T RECOGNIZE THEMSELVES.

THEY WERE AT THEIR WIT'S END. THE SYSTEM HAD FAILED THEM. IT WAS TOO LATE FOR TWEAKS AND REFORMS. THEY WANTED THE WHOLE THING BLOWN TO BITS.

OF COURSE, TRUMP'S SUPPORTERS WEREN'T NAÏVE. THEY DIDN'T AGREE WITH EVERYTHING HE SAID. MANY OF THEM TOOK OFFENSE AT HIS CAUSTIC TONE, BUT THEY OVERLOOKED THAT. TO THEM, TRUMP WAS AN UPTURNED MIDDLE FINGER TO THE POLITICAL ELITE.

THE POWERS THAT BE HAD LONG IGNORED AND SNUBBED THE LITTLE GUY. TRUMP, ON THE OTHER HAND, SPOKE DIRECTLY TO THEM. AND HE WAS TOO LOUD AND RICH AND FAMOUS TO IGNORE.

UNDER A SYSTEM THAT BAILED OUT BILLIONAIRES AND BANKERS, MANY OF TRUMP'S SUPPORTERS WERE THEMSELVES "LOSERS." THEY'D LOST THEIR JOBS, THEIR HOMES, THEIR HOPE, THEIR FAITH IN THE AMERICAN DREAM. UNDER PRESIDENT TRUMP, THEY HOPED, THE COUNTRY'S LUCK -- THEIR LUCK -- WOULD CHANGE.

WE'RE GOING TO **WIN, WIN, WIN!** WE'RE GOING TO WIN SO MUCH, YOU'RE GOING TO GET SICK AND TIRED OF IT. YOU'RE GOING TO SAY, "MR. PRESIDENT, WE CAN'T TAKE IT ANYMORE, WE'RE **WINNING TOO MUCH!"**

SO WHAT IF SPECIAL DEPORTATION SQUADS HAD TO KICK DOWN A FEW MILLION DOORS IN THE DEAD OF NIGHT?

REALITY SHOW

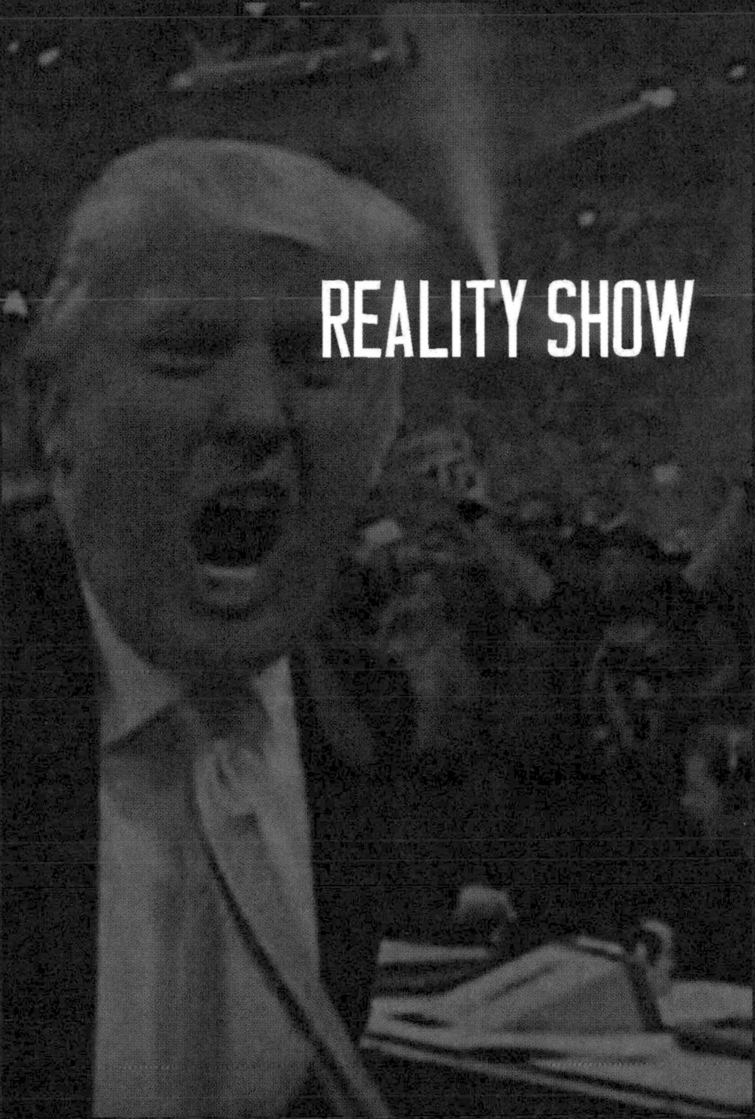

A SMART MAN WHO IS WILLFULLY IGNORANT ABOUT HISTORY? HOW AMERICAN.

TRUMP'S WEALTH AND PREPPY GOOD LOOKS PROPELLED HIM FROM FORTUNE TO FAME VIRTUALLY OVERNIGHT. *THE TODAY SHOW'S* TOM BROKAW INTERVIEWED TRUMP AT AGE 33. IT WAS THE NEW YORKER'S FIRST MAJOR APPEARANCE ON NATIONAL TELEVISION.

AT THE TIME, HIS BROTHER WAS DYING OF ALCOHOLISM.

LIKE DONALD, FRED JR. HAD GONE INTO THE FAMILY BUSINESS. BUT HE LACKED THE KILLER INSTINCT. FRED JR. WANTED TO BE A PILOT, NOT A DEVELOPER.

HE WAS SORT OF CAUGHT IN THE MIDDLE AS SOMEBODY WHO DIDN'T REALLY LOVE IT, AND ONLY BECAUSE HE DIDN'T REALLY LOVE IT, HE WASN'T PARTICULARLY GOOD AT IT.

MY FATHER HAD GREAT CONFIDENCE IN ME, WHICH ... PUT PRESSURE ON FRED.

FRED AND DONALD'S CRITICISM OF FRED JR. WAS RELENTLESS.

FRED JR. DIED IN 1981, AT AGE 42. TRUMP RARELY TALKS ABOUT THE FRED JR. TRAGEDY, BUT IT HELPED SHAPE HIM. "HE WAS A FANTASTIC GUY, BUT HE GOT STUCK ON ALCOHOL," DONALD SAYS.

WATCHING HIS BROTHER'S STRUGGLE WITH ADDICTION CONVINCED HIM TO NEVER TRY CIGARETTES OR START DRINKING.

HE HAD A PROFOUND IMPACT ON MY LIFE, BECAUSE YOU NEVER KNOW WHERE YOU'RE GOING TO END UP.

BY 1985, HE WAS ALREADY FAMOUS ENOUGH TO FEEL THE NEED TO DEFEND HIMSELF FROM HIS CRITICS.

"I believe [the press] make me out to be something more sinister than really I am."

BY 1988, AGE 41, THE TRUMP WE KNOW WAS LARGELY FORMED: CARNIVAL BARKER, BOMBASTIC NATIONALIST, AN AMBITIOUS AND CUNNING MAN WITH A POLITICAL FUTURE WHO DIDN'T LIKE SEEING AMERICA'S PLACE IN THE WORLD IN DECLINE.

WITH THE NEW CENTURY CAME A NEW CAREER:
REALITY TV STAR. FROM 2004 TO 2015,
TRUMP HOSTED *THE APPRENTICE* AND *THE
CELEBRITY APPRENTICE* ON NBC. DURING THE
SAME PERIOD, HE EVEN BECAME A CHARACTER
ON THE BRAZENLY FAKE FARCE THAT IS WWE
PROFESSIONAL WRESTLING.

2007 "BATTLE OF THE BILLIONAIRES"
BETWEEN TRUMP AND VINCE McMAHON

ALL ALONG, PEOPLE WONDERED, WHO IS THE REAL DONALD J. TRUMP?

A WILDLY SUCCESSFUL BUSINESSMAN WHO EMBODIES THE AMERICAN DREAM?

Forbes The World's Billionaires

#324 Donald Trump
Real Time Net Worth As of 5/29/16
$4.5 Billion
Entrepreneur, Personality

Age	69
Source Of Wealth	television, real estate
Self-Made Score	5
Residence	New York, NY
Citizenship	United States

OR A FRAUD WHO GOT RICH THE OLD-FASHIONED WAY (INHERITED IT) AND THEN SQUANDERED HIS SILVER SPOON?

BUSINESS DAY

What's He Really Worth?

FINANCE   DONALD TRUMP

Donald Trump would be richer if he'd have invested in index funds

How Donald Trump Exaggerates And Fibs About His $4.5 Billion Net Worth

TRUMPED: The Donald Has Filed For Bankruptcy Multiple Times. What's His Strategy, and What Can It Teach You?

WHAT ARE HIS POLITICS, REALLY? TRUMP FLIRTS WITH FASCISM. BUT HE'S ALSO AN OUT-OF-THE-BOX POLITICAL THINKER WHO DARES TO QUESTION THE MILITARISM AT THE CORE OF POST-REAGAN REPUBLICANISM.

OBVIOUSLY THE **WAR IN IRAQ** WAS A **BIG FAT MISTAKE**, ALL RIGHT?...THEY **LIED**. THEY SAID THERE WERE WEAPONS OF MASS DESTRUCTION— THERE WERE NONE. AND THEY **KNEW** THERE WERE NONE.

Jeb Bush

Ted Cruz

THE WOMEN

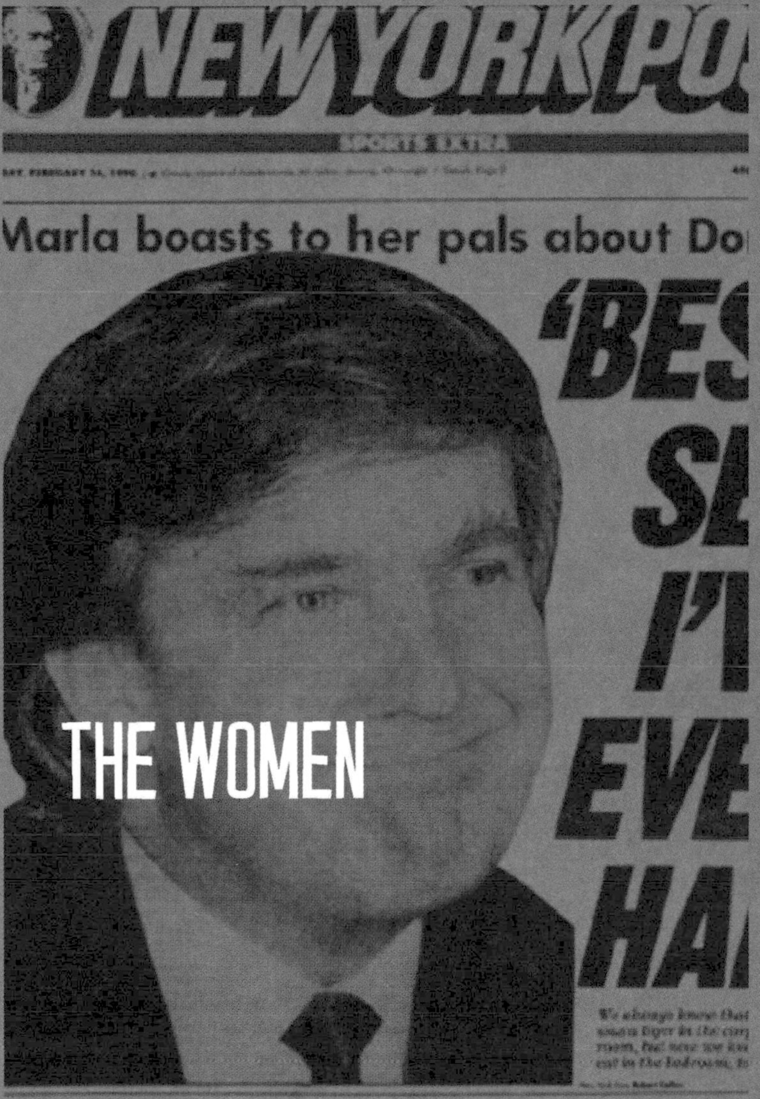
NEW YORK PO
SPORTS EXTRA
Marla boasts to her pals about Do
'BES
SE
I'V
EVE
HA

TRUMP'S RELATIONSHIPS WITH WOMEN ARE RIFE WITH CONTRADICTIONS. HE'S A LOVING FATHER AND FAMILY MAN WHO MANAGES TO GET ALONG WITH HIS EX-WIVES. HE CHOOSES A CERTAIN TYPE OF WOMAN: GLAMOROUS, RITZY, YET ALSO SUBSTANTIAL.

HIS FIRST WIFE, IVANA ZELNIKOVA, WAS A CZECH SKI CHAMPION AND MODEL LIVING IN MONTREAL. SHE MET DONALD WHILE VISITING NEW YORK TO PROMOTE THE MONTREAL WINTER OLYMPIC GAMES. ON APRIL 7, 1977, THEY WERE MARRIED IN A LAVISH SOCIETY WEDDING.

WARM, FEISTY, AND FUNNY, IVANA QUICKLY BECAME A TOP EXECUTIVE WITHIN THE TRUMP ORGANIZATION. SHE WAS APPOINTED VICE PRESIDENT OF INTERIOR DESIGN, THEN PRESIDENT OF THE TRUMP CASTLE HOTEL AND CASINO. SHE OVERSAW THE REMODELING OF NEW YORK'S LANDMARK PLAZA HOTEL, WHERE SHE WAS ALSO PRESIDENT.

DONALD HAD THREE CHILDREN WITH IVANA: DONALD JR., BORN DECEMBER 31, 1977; DAUGHTER IVANKA, BORN OCTOBER 30, 1981; AND ERIC, BORN JANUARY 6, 1984.

IN LATE 1990, HOWEVER, THE TABLOIDS REPORTED THAT DONALD WAS HAVING AN AFFAIR WITH MARLA MAPLES, AN ACTRESS AND FORMER BEAUTY QUEEN FROM GEORGIA. MAPLES CONFRONTED IVANA AT AN ASPEN RESTAURANT DURING A TRUMP FAMILY VACATION.

FOLLOWING THE INEVITABLE MEDIA FEEDING FRENZY, TRUMP PAID TENS OF MILLIONS OF DOLLARS TO IVANA IN A DIVORCE SETTLEMENT. DESPITE EVERYTHING, THE TWO REMAIN FRIENDS. IN APRIL 2008, IVANA MARRIED HER FOURTH HUSBAND AT A LAVISH WEDDING HOSTED BY DONALD AT HIS MAR-A-LAGO RESORT IN FLORIDA.

WE SPEAK BEFORE AND AFTER [HIS CAMPAIGN] APPEARANCES AND HE ASKS ME WHAT I THOUGHT. "BE MORE CALM," I SAY.

TRUMP INSUL

ON OCTOBER 13, 1993, MARLA GAVE BIRTH TO A
DAUGHTER, TIFFANY, NOW 22. THEN, IN DECEMBER
1993, DONALD AND MARLA WERE MARRIED IN FRONT
OF 1,000 GUESTS AT THE PLAZA.

PERHAPS BECAUSE SHE WASN'T QUITE AS
FORMIDABLE AS IVANA, THIS SECOND MARRIAGE
LASTED FEWER THAN FOUR YEARS. ONCE AGAIN,
DONALD'S INFIDELITY WAS PARTLY TO BLAME. BUT
MARLA STILL FEELS FOR HIM.

SHORTLY AFTER HIS 1997 DIVORCE FROM MARLA, DONALD MET MELANIA KNAUSS, A JEWELRY AND WATCH DESIGNER AND FORMER HIGH-FASHION MODEL FROM SLOVENIA. BORN IN 1970 (NOW AGE 45), SHE WAS 25 YEARS YOUNGER THAN DONALD. THIS TIME DONALD DIDN'T RUSH THINGS. AFTER A LONG COURTSHIP, THE TWO WERE MARRIED AT MAR-A-LAGO IN 2005. PUBLICITY-SHY AND INTROVERTED, MELANIA IS REPORTEDLY TRUMP'S EQUAL BEHIND THE SCENES. THIS INCLUDES BEING A SHARP BUSINESSPERSON, AS DEMONSTRATED WHEN SHE LAUNCHED A SUCCESSFUL JEWELRY LINE ON QVC.

MARLA PRAISES DONALD'S FATHERING.

SHE KNOWS HER DAD LOVES HER.

SEEMING TO CONFIRM THAT DONALD RESPECTS THE WOMEN AROUND HIM, HIS DAUGHTER IVANKA, 34, IS HIS MOST TRUSTED BUSINESS PARTNER AND POLITICAL ADVISOR.

THAT'S WHAT WE KNOW OF HIS RELATIONSHIPS WITH WOMEN IN HIS PERSONAL LIFE. IN PUBLIC, SEXIST BILE AND MACHO BRAGGADOCIO SPEWED LIKE OLD FAITHFUL.

1991

"IT DOESN'T REALLY MATTER WHAT [THE MEDIA] WRITE AS LONG AS YOU'VE GOT A YOUNG AND BEAUTIFUL PIECE OF ASS."

1997

"I'VE BEEN SO LUCKY IN TERMS OF [STDs LIKE HIV/AIDS]... IT IS MY PERSONAL VIETNAM. I FEEL LIKE A GREAT AND VERY BRAVE SOLDIER."

2015

"LOOK AT THAT FACE! WOULD ANYONE VOTE FOR THAT?" [ABOUT CARLY FIORINA]

NORMA FOERDERER, TRUMP VICE PRESIDENT AND HIS RIGHT-HAND PERSON FOR 26 YEARS, CLAIMS THAT HER OLD BOSS WAS SUPPORTIVE OF HER AND OTHER WOMEN. SHE SAYS THERE ARE TWO DONALD TRUMPS:

DONALD CAN BE TOTALLY **OUTRAGEOUS**, BUT... IN A WONDERFUL WAY THAT GETS HIM COVERAGE. THAT PERSONA SELLS HIS LICENSED PRODUCTS AND HIS CONDOMINIUMS...
[BUT IN PRIVATE, HE'S] THE DEAREST, MOST THOUGHTFUL, MOST LOYAL, MOST CARING MAN.

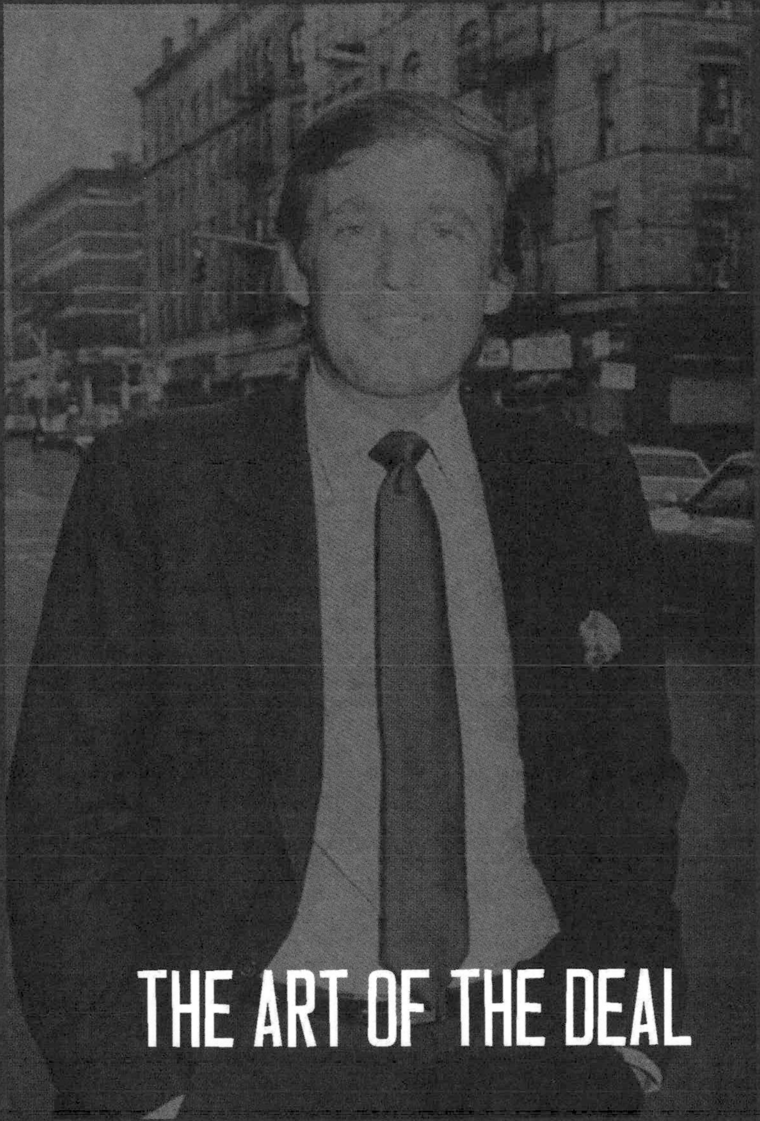
THE ART OF THE DEAL

NO ONE IS WITHOUT CONTRADICTIONS. BUT WITH DONALD JOHN TRUMP, THE CONTRASTS ARE STARTLING -- WHETHER IT'S HIS PERSONAL LIFE OR HIS POLITICAL PERSONA. CONSIDER, FOR EXAMPLE, HIS VIEWS ON OBAMA'S AFFORDABLE CARE ACT.

WE'RE GOING TO REPEAL OBAMA-CARE... [BUT] YOU'RE NOT GOING TO LET PEOPLE DIE SITTING IN THE MIDDLE OF THE STREET.

LIVE

LIVE
①NEWS

REPUBLICAN PRESIDENTIAL DEBATE

EXTREMISM, REASON, EMPATHY. ALL IN THE SAME BREATH.

SOMETIMES HE COMES OFF LIKE THE "IDIOTS" HE DECRIES.

Trump on a visit to the *New York Times*:

"But certainly cyber has to be a, you know, certainly cyber has to be in our thought process, very strongly in our thought process. Inconceivable that, inconceivable the power of cyber. But as you say, you can take out, you can take out, you can make countries nonfunctioning with a strong use of cyber."

IS THERE A METHOD TO THE MADNESS?

"I don't want to say what I'd do because, again, we need unpredictability. You know, if I win, I don't want to be in a position where I've said I would or I wouldn't. I don't want them to know what I'm thinking."

MAYBE HE'S JUST WINGING IT.

THAT SEEMED TO BE
THE CASE IN 2011, WHEN
TRUMP PICKED UP THE
MANTLE OF THE
BIRTHER MOVEMENT,
WHICH ACCUSED
OBAMA OF HAVING
BEEN BORN IN KENYA
AND THUS BEING
DISQUALIFIED FROM
HOLDING THE OFFICE
OF PRESIDENT. TRUMP'S
INVOLVEMENT
PROMPTED THE MEDIA
TO BEGIN COVERING
RUMORS THAT HAD
BEEN CIRCULATING
ONLINE SINCE 2008.

TRUMP HAD NO
EVIDENCE FOR HIS
CLAIMS. NONETHELESS,
THE PRESIDENT FELT
ENOUGH PRESSURE
FROM TRUMP TO
FINALLY ORDER THE
RELEASE OF HIS
HAWAIIAN LONG-FORM
BIRTH CERTIFICATE.

TRUMP'S BESTSELLING 1987 BOOK, *THE ART OF THE DEAL*, REVEALS THE BUSINESSMAN'S APPROACH. HE ACQUIRES. HE DUMPS. HE LURKS, WAITING FOR A GOOD OPPORTUNITY.

LOSSES ARE TO BE LEARNED FROM.

NOVEMBER 2012: TRUMP CONDUCTED A QUICK ELECTION POSTMORTEM. WHY HAD MITT ROMNEY LOST? IT WAS SO OBVIOUS: BECAUSE HE WAS "WEAK."

IF YOU LOOK AT ROMNEY, NOW ROMNEY CHOKED, OK? HE CHOKED LIKE A DOG. HE SHOULD HAVE **WON** THAT. THAT WAS AN ELECTION THAT SHOULD HAVE BEEN WON.

morning joe **msnbc**

SAM NUNBERG, REPUBLICAN STRATEGIST FOR TRUMP, 2013-2015: "I DON'T THINK PEOPLE REALIZED HE HAS ALWAYS HAD PRESIDENTIAL ASPIRATIONS. HE KNOWS THE VOTERS HE ATTRACTS. HE KNEW IT FROM THE BEGINNING."

BEYOND HIS CONTEMPT FOR ROMNEY, TRUMP SAW AN OPENING. IF AMERICANS WANTED A STRONG LEADER, SOMEONE UNSCRIPTED, SOMEONE WHO TELLS IT LIKE IT IS, DAMN THE CONSEQUENCES, HE WAS THEIR MAN.

HE TOLD HIS STAFF TO RAMP UP.

"MAKE AMERICA GREAT AGAIN," OK?

THAT'S OUR SLOGAN. REGISTER THE TRADE-MARK. TIME FOR MY KIDS TO STEP UP, RUN THE BUSINESS MORE, SO I CAN FOCUS ON 2016.

HE'D FIGURE OUT THE PESKY DETAILS — BALLOT ACCESS, DELEGATE RULES, HOW TO NAVIGATE THE DIFFERENT LAWS GOVERNING EACH STATE'S ELECTION APPARATUS, NOT TO MENTION HIS OWN POLICIES AND ISSUES — LATER.

CANDIDATE

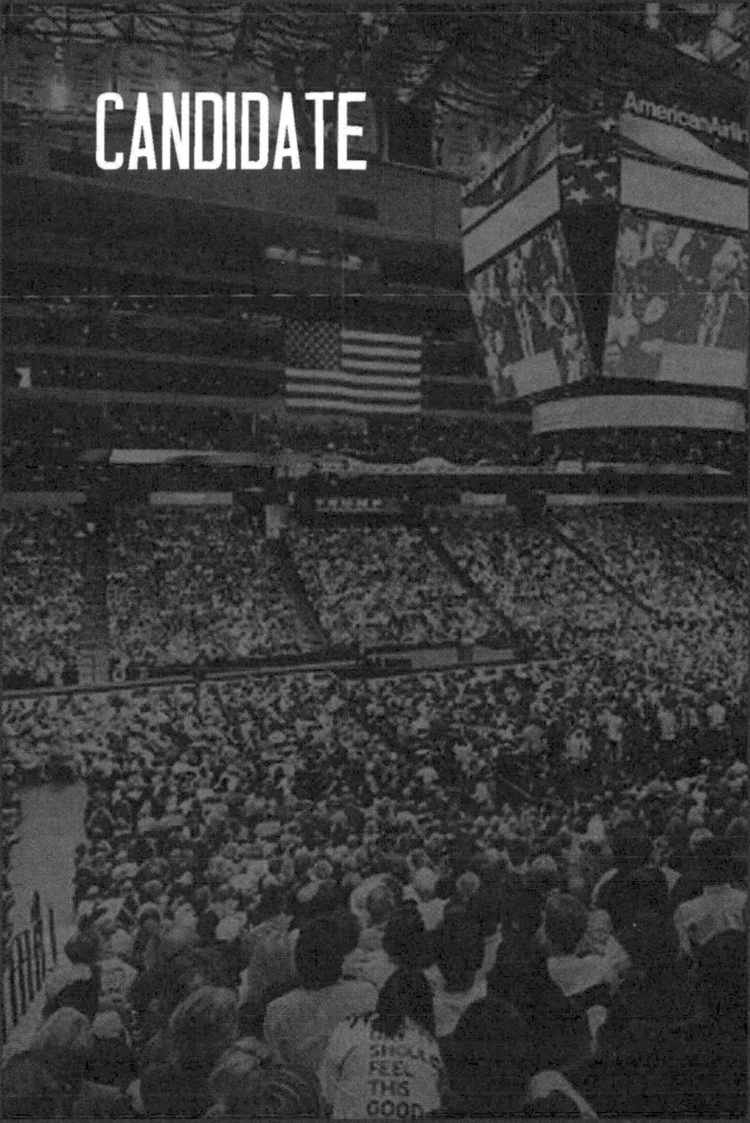

 **KYLE SMITH**

NEWS

Stop pretending — Donald Trump is not running for president

By Kyle Smith   May 30, 2015

BY HIS 60s, TRUMP HAD ACQUIRED A REPUTATION FOR SAYING THINGS HE DIDN'T MEAN. SO WHEN HE ANNOUNCED HIS CAMPAIGN FOR THE 2016 REPUBLICAN PRESIDENTIAL NOMINATION, MOST PUNDITS THOUGHT IT WAS JUST ANOTHER FAKE-OUT, A PUBLICITY STUNT TO PROMOTE HIS BOOKS AND HIS BRAND.

IT WOULDN'T HAVE BEEN THE FIRST TIME HE PRETENDED TO RUN FOR PRESIDENT.

YOU THINK GORBACHEV* IS TOUGH, THINK OF THIS CHARACTER KHOMEINI!** I MEAN THIS SON OF A BITCH IS SOMETHING LIKE NOBODY'S EVER SEEN. HE MAKES GORBACHEV LOOK LIKE A BABY. AND GORBACHEV IS ONE TOUGH COOKIE.

* PRESIDENT OF THE SOVIET UNION

** SUPREME LEADER OF IRAN

DRAF
TRUM

1987

HE DID IT AGAIN IN 2004, AND 2012.

LOOKING BACK NOW, TRUMP'S MESSAGE OVER THE YEARS WAS ALWAYS THE SAME: AMERICA COULD DO BETTER. ITS LEADERS ARE WEAK. WE NEED A STRONGMAN: HIM.

I AM OFFICIALLY RUNNING FOR PRESIDENT OF THE UNITED STATES, AND WE ARE GOING TO MAKE OUR COUNTRY GREAT AGAIN.

SADLY THE AMERICAN DREAM IS **DEAD**. BUT... I WILL BRING IT BACK BIGGER AND BETTER AND STRONGER THAN...BEFORE.

JUNE 17, 2015

TRUMP

www.DonaldJTrump.com

MAKE AMERICA GREAT AGAIN

BUT THIS TIME HE SEEMED MORE SERIOUS.

McCAIN

TRUMP'S FIRST MAJOR POLICY PRONOUNCEMENT WAS UNORIGINAL. ARIZONA SENATOR JOHN McCAIN HAD ONCE PROMISED TO BUILD A "BERLIN WALL" ALONG THE BORDER WITH MEXICO. TO THIS IDEA, TRUMP ADDED PANACHE: HE'D FORCE THE MEXICANS TO PAY FOR IT.

AUGUST 19, 2015

AS YOU KNOW, I KNOW HOW TO BUILD. I KNOW HOW TO GET IT DONE. WE'LL HAVE A GREAT WALL. WE'LL CALL IT THE GREAT WALL OF TRUMP. WE'LL HAVE A GREAT WALL AND IT'LL BE — IT'LL BE ACTUALLY — IT CAN BE A GOOD-LOOKING WALL, AS WALLS GO, BUT WE'LL HAVE A REALLY TERRIFIC WALL AND IT'LL BE DONE FOR THE RIGHT PRICE.

I'M NOT GOING TO PAY FOR THAT FUCK-ING WALL.

Vicente Fox, ex-President of Mexico

94

ESTABLISHMENT JOURNALISTS SCOFFED. BY 2015, THE POPULATION OF ILLEGAL IMMIGRANTS FROM MEXICO WAS DECREASING -- DUE TO THE LOUSY ECONOMY, MORE WERE LEAVING HERE THAN ARRIVING. YET POLLS QUICKLY SHOWED TRUMP TIED FOR FIRST PLACE WITH FORMER FLORIDA GOVERNOR JEB BUSH, THE ESTABLISHMENT FAVORITE AT THE TIME.

IT WAS A STRONG START -- BUT THEN TRUMP COMMITTED A ROOKIE MISTAKE. HE ATTACKED AN UNTOUCHABLE FIGURE.

FOR ANY OTHER PRESIDENTIAL CANDIDATE, EVEN IF
HE'D APOLOGIZED AFTERWARD, INSULTING A
DECORATED P.O.W. TORTURED AT THE "HANOI
HILTON" DURING THE VIETNAM WAR WOULD HAVE
DOOMED HIS CAMPAIGN. BUT TRUMP WASN'T MOST
CANDIDATES. IN WHAT WOULD SOON BECOME A
TREND, HE DIDN'T WALK IT BACK, MUCH LESS
APOLOGIZE. HE DOUBLED DOWN.

> "I think John McCain's done very
> little for the veterans. I'm very
> disappointed in John McCain. He's
> yet another all talk, no action
> politician who spends too much
> time on television and not enough
> time doing his job."

TRUMP'S GAMBLE PAID OFF. AS HE'D GUESSED,
McCAIN WAS A PAPER TIGER. THE ONLY PEOPLE WHO
WORSHIPPED McCAIN WERE D.C. INSIDERS -- AND THEY
DIDN'T VOTE IN REPUBLICAN PRIMARIES.

EVEN AS HE CLIMBED IN THE POLLS, REPUBLICAN STRATEGISTS ASSUMED THE TRUMP CAMPAIGN WAS A SPECULATIVE BUBBLE THAT WOULD INEVITABLY BURST. HE WAS SIMPLY TOO OUTRAGEOUS. HIS RHETORIC WAS TOO VAGUE. HE WASN'T *PRESIDENTIAL*.

Rick Wilson, July 2015:

"The circus is almost over. My advice to Trump fans? Don't be the last clown out of the tent."

THE EXPERTS WERE OUT OF TOUCH WITH A BIG SWATH OF THE AMERICAN PEOPLE. THE MORE TRUMP PISSED OFF THE ESTABLISHMENT MEDIA AND POLITICIANS, THE MORE HE ENDEARED HIMSELF TO ORDINARY REPUBLICANS.

NOW, TO THE DELIGHT OF HIS FANS -- AND THE MEDIA -- TRUMP TURNED HIS GIFT FOR ATTACK TO THE OTHER CONTENDERS.

"LYIN' TED"
TX sen. TED CRUZ

SHE GOT SCHLONGED!
"CROOKED HILLARY"
ex-secy. of state HILLARY CLINTON

ALL REPUBLICAN CANDIDATES LAMBASTED THE GOVERNMENT AS INCOMPETENT AND WASTEFUL. ALL OF THEM ARGUED THAT THERE WAS NO ROOM FOR COMPROMISE WITH THE DEMOCRATS. ALL OF THEM SPOKE GRAVELY ABOUT THE SUPPOSED THREAT PRESENTED BY ILLEGAL IMMIGRANTS "STREAMING ACROSS THE BORDER."

THAT STUFF WAS BOILERPLATE.

BUT TRUMP WENT FURTHER. HE AGREED WITH THE PRESCRIPTION, SURE. BUT THEN HE OFFERED A RADICAL SOLUTION, WHICH HE DILUTED TO A PITHY MONOSYLLABIC BUMPER STICKER: BUILD THE WALL. PEOPLE BOUGHT INTO IT. NOT DESPITE HIS WILD TONE, BUT BECAUSE IT SIGNIFIED HIS TRUE MAVERICK STATUS.

Jonathan Freedland, The Guardian

Through the intensity of Republicans' anti-government rhetoric, their disdain for compromise and the very business of politics, and their indulgence of bigoted attitudes to immigration, [the Republicans] rolled the pitch on which Trump is now playing.

ON OTHER ISSUES, TRUMP REJECTED OR RETHOUGHT THE REPUBLICAN PARTY LINE. WHEN HE SAID HE PREFERRED DIPLOMACY WITH ADVERSARIES LIKE IRAN AND RUSSIA OVER WAR -- AND TALKING OVER BOMBING -- GOP PUNDITS ASSUMED VOTERS WOULD REJECT HIM. ON THE CONTRARY.

IF WE GET ALONG WELL WITH RUSSIA, THAT'S A POSITIVE THING, NOT A NEGATIVE THING.

TRUMP ATTACKED THAT NEO-CON GOP STAPLE, "REGIME CHANGE," MORE FEROCIOUSLY THAN ANY DEMOCRAT:

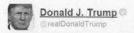
Donald J. Trump ⊘
@realDonaldTrump

Jeb, why did your brother attack and destabalize the Middle East by attacking Iraq when there were no weapons of mass destruction? Bad info?

TRUMP: I WAS ALWAYS OPPOSED TO IRAQ WAR

"Look at Libya. Look at Iraq. Iraq used to be no terrorists. [Saddam Hussein] would kill the terrorists immediately, which is like now it's the Harvard of terrorism. If you look at Iraq from years ago, I'm not saying he was a nice guy, he was a horrible guy, but it was a lot better than it is right now. Right now, Iraq is a training ground for terrorists. Right now Libya, nobody even knows Libya, frankly there is no Iraq and there is no Libya. It's all broken up."

TRUMP CHALLENGED THE LONG-DOMINANT CORPORATIST WING OF THE GOP. HE TAPPED INTO ANGER OVER JOB-KILLING TRADE DEALS LIKE NAFTA, SUPPORTED BY BOTH PARTIES:

IT'S A DISASTER... WE WILL EITHER RENEGOTIATE IT, OR WE WILL BREAK IT. BECAUSE, YOU KNOW, EVERY AGREEMENT HAS AN END.

WAS THIS GUY REALLY A REPUBLICAN? EVEN BERNIE SANDERS WASN'T AS CONTEMPTUOUS OF "FREE TRADE."

PERHAPS THE BIGGEST SHOCK TO THE BUSINESS BLOC WAS HIS POPULIST APPROACH TO TAXES. HE SAID HE WAS WILLING TO RAISE TAXES ON THE RICH:

THE HEDGE FUND PEOPLE MAKE A LOT OF MONEY AND THEY PAY VERY LITTLE TAX. I WANT TO LOWER TAXES FOR THE MIDDLE CLASS... I DON'T MIND PAYING A LITTLE MORE IN TAXES.

PARTY INSIDERS' HEADS SPUN, BUT THE CROWDS LOVED IT.

HE BROKE THE MOLD ON SOCIAL ISSUES TOO. LATER IN THE RACE, TRUMP CRITICIZED A NEW NORTH CAROLINA "BATHROOM LAW" THAT TARGETED TRANSGENDER PEOPLE AND DEFENDED THE RIGHT OF PEOPLE TO USE ANY PUBLIC RESTROOM THEY WANT.

HE SAID HE THOUGHT MARRIAGE SHOULD BE BETWEEN A MAN AND A WOMAN, BUT HE HAS HIRED GAYS AND LESBIANS IN HIGH-PROFILE POSITIONS AND CONSISTENTLY DEFENDED LGBT PEOPLE.

HE WILL BE THE **MOST** GAY-FRIENDLY REPUBLICAN NOMINEE FOR PRESIDENT **EVER**.

Gregory Angelo, President, Log Cabin Republicans

GOD, GAYS, AND GUNS -- TRUMP LIKES GUNS, BUT HE IS AN APOSTATE ON AT LEAST A THIRD OF THE REPUBLICAN HOLY TRINITY. (MORE LIKE TWO OUT OF THREE, SINCE HE ISN'T RELIGIOUS.)

ALL THESE STANCES, WE'D BEEN TOLD FOR AS LONG AS ANYONE COULD REMEMBER, WOULD NEVER FLY WITH REPUBLICAN VOTERS. YET HERE WAS DONALD TRUMP, WINNING ONE PRIMARY AFTER ANOTHER, AND BY BIG MARGINS. THE REPUBLICAN PARTY, TRUMP PROVED, DIDN'T REALLY KNOW WHAT REPUBLICAN VOTERS WANTED OR CARED ABOUT.

THIS IS ABSOLUTELY A CRISIS FOR THE PARTY ELITE — AND, BEYOND THE PARTY ELITE, FOR ELECTED OFFICIALS, AND FOR THE WAY PEOPLE HAVE BEEN RAISED AS REPUBLICANS IN THE POWER STRUCTURE FOR A GENERATION.

Ari Fleischer, press secy. for George W. Bush

THANKS TO TRUMP AND HIS SNIDE ASIDES AND
CONSTANT INTERRUPTIONS, THE REPUBLICAN
DEBATES DEVOLVED INTO INFANTILE
NAME-CALLING AND INCOHERENT RANTS.

BUT THEY WERE NEVER BORING.

EVEN WITH ALL THOSE OTHER BOLDFACE
SENATORS AND GOVERNORS STANDING TO HIS
LEFT AND RIGHT, DONALD TRUMP'S CHARISMA
STOOD OUT.

IT OFTEN FELT LIKE HE WAS THE ONLY ONE ON
THE STAGE.

TRUMP'S STYLE WASN'T LIKE ANY OTHER POLITICIAN'S. NO TELEPROMPTERS FOR HIM. NOT EVEN CHEAT CARDS.

HIS SPEECHES WERE COMPLETELY AD-LIBBED, OFF THE CUFF.

IF A LINE FELL FLAT, HE TURNED ON A DIME AND HEADED OFF IN ANOTHER, SOMETIMES TOTALLY OPPOSITE, DIRECTION. YET DESPITE HIS HIGH-SPEED FLIP-FLOPS, TRUMP'S OVERALL STRATEGY WAS CAREFULLY CONTRIVED TO FILL A CHASM IN THE MARKETPLACE OF IDEAS.

> "His wall proposal had been hatched earlier as an idea uniting his role as a builder with a hard-line stance on immigration."
>
> —*Wall Street Journal*

THERE WAS A METHOD BEHIND THE MADNESS.

DONALD TRUMP WAS ENGAGED IN ONE OF THE BIGGEST PROJECTS OF HIS CAREER: A HOSTILE TAKEOVER OF THE REPUBLICAN PARTY, AND THE PRESIDENCY.

HE WASN'T MERELY WILLING TO BREAK SOME RULES. HE KNEW HE COULDN'T WIN UNLESS HE COMPLETELY SHATTERED THE BASIC ASSUMPTIONS OF WHAT AMERICANS WANTED IN A LEADER.

THE ACCIDENTAL
AUTHORITARIAN

COLUMBIA UNIVERSITY HISTORY PROFESSOR
ROBERT PAXTON WROTE THE BOOK ON
FASCISM. LITERALLY.

YEARS BEFORE HE
WROTE THAT
BOOK, HE'D
WRITTEN THE BOOK
ON THE NAZI
OCCUPATION OF
FRANCE. IT WAS SO
SUCCESSFUL THAT
IT BECAME THE
URTEXT ON VICHY
IN FRANCE.

AS A STUDENT
AT COLUMBIA, I
WAS THRILLED
TO GET INTO
PAXTON'S
SEMINAR ON
FASCISM.

ASIDE FROM CLASS PARTICIPATION, THERE WAS JUST ONE GRADED ASSIGNMENT IN PAXTON'S CLASS: A PAPER BASED ON ONE QUESTION.

TO WHICH COUNTRY IS **FASCISM** MOST LIKELY TO COME TODAY, AND WHY?

Final paper due Dec. 23

I ANSWERED "THE UNITED STATES" AND SET OUT TO MAKE MY CASE. I KNEW IT WAS A CONTROVERSIAL CHOICE. STILL, HE GAVE ME AN "A" -- AND HE WAS A TOUGH GRADER. SO WHAT DOES PAXTON, NOW RETIRED, THINK OF TRUMP?

IF AND WHEN FASCISM COMES HERE, IT WILL BE IN AN ALL-AMERICAN FORM: CHRISTIAN. COUNTRIFIED. MAYBE AN ATHLETE.

CLASSIC FASCISM DURING THE 20TH CENTURY
AROSE IN NATIONS WHERE DEMOCRATIC
GOVERNANCE EITHER HAD FAILED OR WAS
WIDELY PERCEIVED TO HAVE FAILED.

THE TEXTBOOK EXAMPLE WAS THE WEIMAR
REPUBLIC IN GERMANY DURING THE 1920s.

"[Weimar is] lacking any ideas... [and is] not led but administered by a bureaucratic caste."

Carl von Ossietzsky

German Pacifist

1924

"Neither party is in a position to negotiate political compromises."

Harold Pollack

The Politico

TECHNOCRATS HAVE RUN THE U.S. SYSTEM FOR
DECADES. MOREOVER, BECAUSE THE U.S.
CONGRESS AND THE PRESIDENCY HAVE BEEN
CONTROLLED BY DIFFERENT PARTIES IN RECENT
YEARS, GRIDLOCK HAS EVEN PREVENTED
ROUTINE BUSINESS LIKE JUDICIAL APPOINT-
MENTS AND BUDGETS FROM BEING APPROVED.

TODAY (2016), 11% OF AMERICANS APPROVE
OF CONGRESS.

GERMANY, 1933:
CONSERVATIVE AUTHORITARIANISM
GAVE WAY TO DICTATORSHIP IN A
COUNTRY THAT WAS ON ITS KNEES
ECONOMICALLY, ITS MORALE CRUSHED.
FROM THE HARD RIGHT, THERE WAS
FEAR-MONGERING, BLAMING THE JEWS
AND OTHER FOREIGN ELEMENTS FOR
AILMENTS THEY HAD LITTLE TO DO
WITH, AN INSISTENCE ON THE
GREATNESS OF THE GERMAN PEOPLE --
A DESTINY STOLEN FROM THEM BY A
MYTHICAL "STAB IN THE BACK" FROM
WITHIN THAT SUPPOSEDLY CAUSED
THEM TO LOSE WORLD WAR I.

AFTER A DECADE OF TEETERING, INCOMPETENT PARLIAMENTARY DEMOCRACY, GERMANS WERE EXHAUSTED. THEY WERE SICK OF LIVING IN A NATION IN DECLINE, TIRED OF BEING AFRAID, READY TO BLAME SOMEONE -- ANYONE -- FOR SCREWING THEM OVER. THE NAZIS' CULT OF THE LEADER, THE ONE BRILLIANT MAN OF STEEL READY, WILLING, AND ABLE TO SOLVE THE NATION'S PROBLEMS, LOOKED LIKE THE SOLUTION.

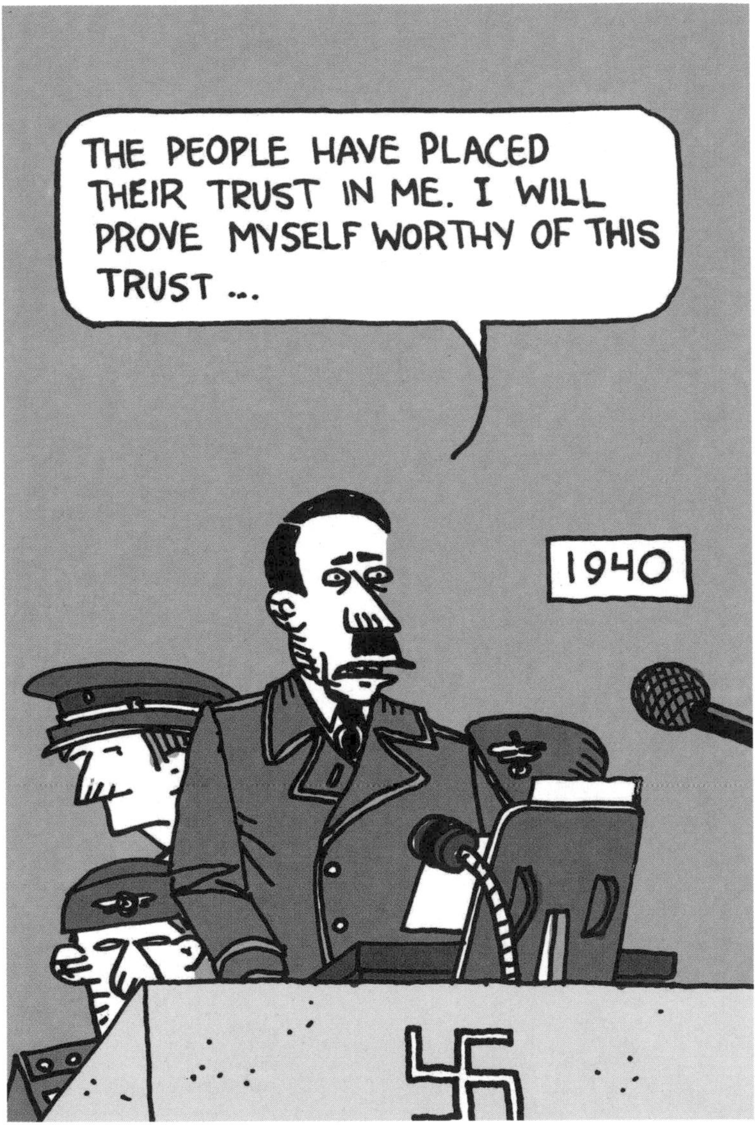
THE PEOPLE HAVE PLACED THEIR TRUST IN ME. I WILL PROVE MYSELF WORTHY OF THIS TRUST ...
1940

TRUMP MADE NO SECRET OF HIS ADMIRATION FOR NATION-STATES THAT PUT THEIR OWN INTERESTS AHEAD OF THEIR CITIZENS'.

WHEN THE STUDENTS POURED INTO TIANANMEN SQUARE, THE CHINESE GOVERNMENT ALMOST BLEW IT, THEY WERE **VICIOUS**, THEY WERE **BRUTAL**, AND THEN' THEY PUT IT DOWN WITH **STRENGTH**. THAT SHOWS YOU THE **POWER** OF **STRENGTH**.

THERE ARE PARALLELS BETWEEN FASCISM AND TRUMPISM. AND DIFFERENCES.

THIS THING ABOUT THE **STRONG STATE**, AND EVERYBODY REGIMENTED, AND WEARING **UNIFORMS**, THE SHIRTS THE SAME COLOR, ARMS OUT THE SAME WAY— THIS IS NOT THE STYLE OF AMERICANS.

Robert Paxton

TRUMP HAS CALLED HIMSELF A "MILITARIST" --
THAT'S AT THE CORE OF CLASSIC FASCISM --
BUT HE PROBABLY DOESN'T KNOW WHAT THE
WORD REALLY MEANS. AND HE FAMOUSLY
OPPOSED THE 2003 INVASION OF IRAQ.

IT'S ONE OF THE WORST DECISIONS IN THE HISTORY OF THE COUNTRY.

DEFEAT ISIS BY TAKING THEIR WEALTH. TAKE BACK THE OIL... BOMB THE HELL OUT OF THEM.

IF YOU'RE A PACIFIST, DON'T BE TOO
QUICK TO EMBRACE TRUMP. HE'S
PERFECTLY WILLING TO START NEW WARS.

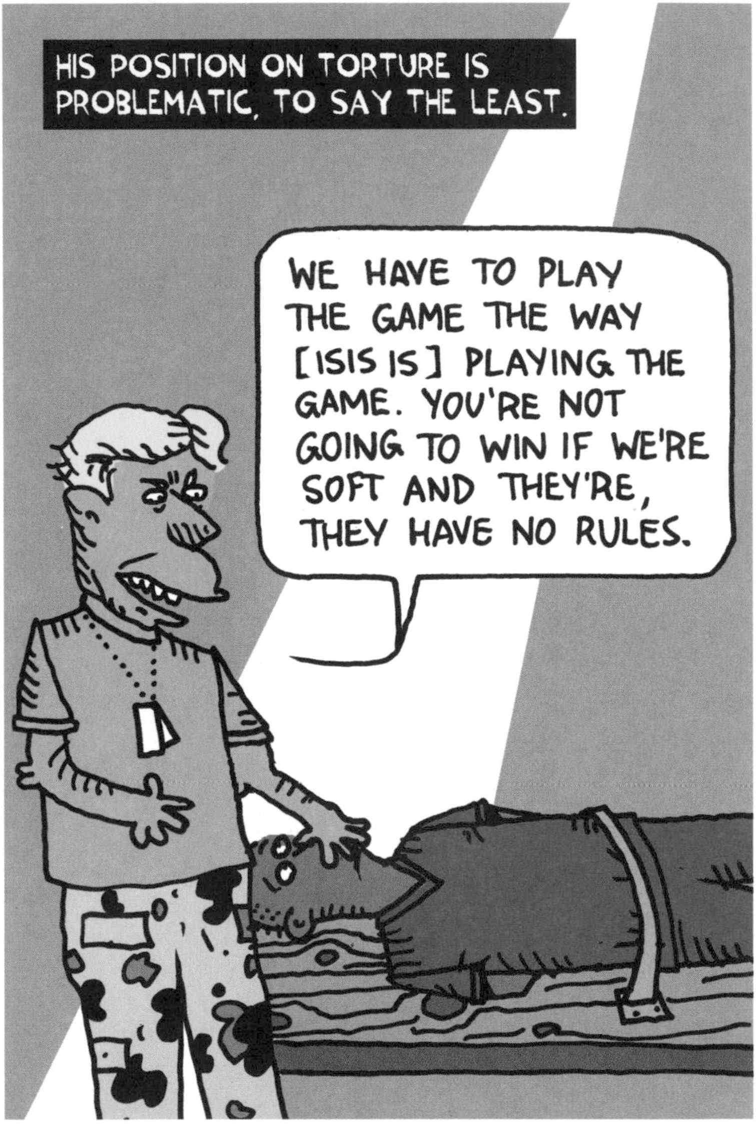
HIS POSITION ON TORTURE IS PROBLEMATIC, TO SAY THE LEAST.
WE HAVE TO PLAY THE GAME THE WAY [ISIS IS] PLAYING THE GAME. YOU'RE NOT GOING TO WIN IF WE'RE SOFT AND THEY'RE, THEY HAVE NO RULES.

PAXTON: "MY IMPRESSION . . . IS THAT HE'S
A BLUSTERY, EGOCENTRIC BLOWHARD. AND
THIS COMES NATURALLY TO HIM AND IT HAS
WORKED. HE HAS AN INSTINCT FOR FEARS
AND ANGER OUT IN THE PUBLIC AND HE
MATCHES UP WITH THEM PERFECTLY. I DON'T
THINK OF TRUMP AS A MAN WHO'S STUDIED
MUCH OF ANYTHING. HE'S VERY
SPONTANEOUS; HE HAS A GENIUS FOR
SENSING THE MOOD OF A CROWD AND I
THINK TO SOME DEGREE HITLER AND
MUSSOLINI HAD THOSE QUALITIES ALSO. I
DO NOT THINK HE'S LEARNED THIS FROM A
BOOK."

IN *THE ART OF THE DEAL* TRUMP HINTS AT WHY HE LOVES BOMBAST: IT'S EFFECTIVE. IT ALSO GIVES YOU COVER.

THERE'S NO WAY, LISTENERS ASSUME, THAT YOU COULD POSSIBLY MEAN EVERYTHING YOU SAY. BUT THEN, IF IT TURNS OUT YOU DID, NOBODY CAN CLAIM THEY WEREN'T WARNED.

I PLAY TO PEOPLE'S **FANTASIES**. PEOPLE MAY NOT ALWAYS THINK BIG THEMSELVES, BUT THEY CAN STILL GET VERY EXCITED BY THOSE WHO DO. THAT'S WHY A LITTLE **HYPERBOLE** NEVER HURTS.

UNLESS YOU'RE IN IRAQ, WHICH WAS DESTROYED BY A WAR SOLD USING HYPERBOLE.

TRUMP CAN SEEM LIKEABLE. FUNNY.
HILARIOUS, EVEN.

MUSSOLINI HAD REMARKABLE
CHARISMA TOO.

HITLER COULD BE FUNNY, EVEN
DROLL.

POINT IS, DEALMAKERS AND MASTER
SALESMEN LIKE TRUMP ALL HAVE
THAT PERSUASIVE POWER. HE
APPEALS ON A VISCERAL LEVEL
BECAUSE HE SEEMS REAL.

IS TRUMP FASCIST? PROTOFASCIST?

LET'S HOPE WE NEVER HAVE TO FIND
OUT.

WHAT WE DO KNOW IS THAT HE IS
DEPLOYING FASCIST TACTICS. HE
FITS THE MOLD.

"CUT FROM A DIFFERENT CLOTH"

WHEN 20-YEAR-OLD DONALD TRUMP ARRIVED AT WHARTON, HE WAS DISAPPOINTED THAT HIS CLASSMATES WEREN'T AS SHARP AS HE'D EXPECTED.

"IN MY OPINION, THAT [WHARTON] DEGREE DOESN'T PROVE VERY MUCH, BUT A LOT OF PEOPLE I DO BUSINESS WITH TAKE IT VERY SERIOUSLY, AND IT'S CONSIDERED VERY PRESTIGIOUS."

— The Art of the Deal

TRUMP MAINTAINED SUCH A LOW PROFILE AT U. PENN. THAT SOME CLASSMATES DOUBT HE WAS REALLY THERE. (HE WAS.) TRUTH WAS, HIS MIND WAS ALREADY ON BUSINESS.

TRUMP DIDN'T TAKE ACADEMICS SERIOUSLY.
HIS CLASSMATE LOUIS CALOMARIS
REMEMBERS:

"DON WAS A BRIGHT GUY, BUT
I'D SAY A DISINTERESTED
STUDENT. WHAT HE WAS REALLY
INTERESTED IN WAS HOW TO
MAKE DEALS, AND LEVERAGE
FINANCING. HE WAS ALWAYS
LOOKING FOR THE QUICK DEAL,
THE FAST KILL. HE LOOKED
WITH DISDAIN AT THE **GRUNT
WORK**.

I COULD TELL HALF
THE TIME HE DIDN'T
READ THE ASSIGN-
MENT. HE'D **BLUFF
HIS WAY THROUGH
IT**."

1968 WAS A WATERSHED YEAR IN HISTORY: THE TET OFFENSIVE, THE RFK AND MLK ASSASSINATIONS, THE STUDENT TAKEOVER AT COLUMBIA AND THE PARIS UPRISING.

COLLEGE CAMPUSES WERE CENTERS OF INTENSE POLITICAL DEBATE. THE WAR IN VIETNAM WAS A MAJOR TOPIC OF DISCUSSION AT COLLEGES AND UNIVERSITIES LIKE U. PENN. MOREOVER, PHILADELPHIA WAS A HOTBED OF RACIAL TENSION. BUT TRUMP DIDN'T ENGAGE WITH THE GREAT ISSUES OF THE TIME.

I WASN'T A FAN OF THE VIETNAM WAR, THAT I CAN TELL YOU. BUT I WASN'T A MARCHER.

WHILE IN COLLEGE, TRUMP QUALIFIED FOR DEFERMENTS SO HE WOULDN'T HAVE TO GO TO VIETNAM. JUST AFTER GRADUATION, A FRIENDLY DOCTOR WROTE HIM A MEDICAL DEFERMENT FOR "BONE SPURS."

A CAREERIST DETERMINED TO FOLLOW IN HIS FATHER'S FOOTSTEPS AS A DEVELOPER, HE FOCUSED ON WORK -- AND HIS IMAGE (TODAY WE'D CALL IT HIS BRAND). ACTRESS CANDICE BERGEN, WHO ATTENDED WHARTON AT THE TIME, REMEMBERS GOING ON A BLIND DATE WITH TRUMP.

I JUST REMEMBER THAT HE WAS WEARING A THREE-PIECE BURGUNDY SUIT, AND BURGUNDY BOOTS AND [HAD A CHAUFFEUR-DRIVEN] BURGUNDY LIMOUSINE.

HE WAS VERY COORDINATED.

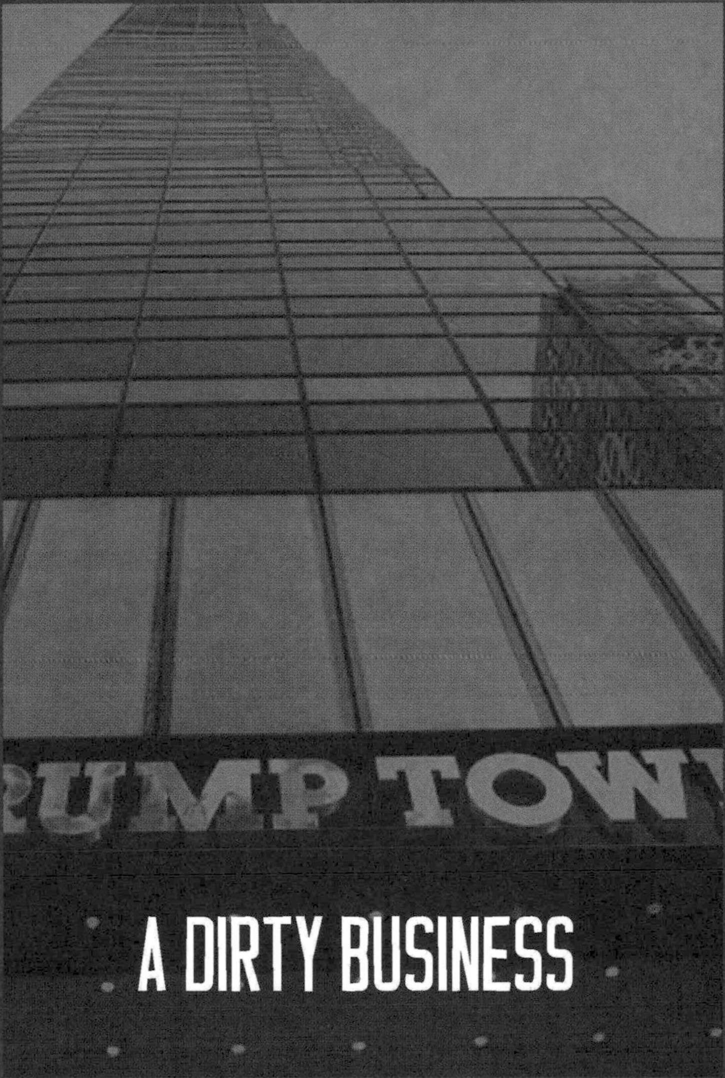

A DIRTY BUSINESS

REAL ESTATE IS A NASTY BUSINESS. YOU CHARGE PEOPLE WHO NEED SHELTER MORE RENT THAN A SPACE IS WORTH, OR SELL THEM PROPERTY FOR MORE THAN YOU PAID -- WHICH MAKES EVERYTHING MORE EXPENSIVE FOR EVERYONE ELSE WHO LIVES NEARBY.

A DEVELOPER MUST SET ASIDE HIS SCRUPLES. BECAUSE HE MUST CULTIVATE CLOSE RELATIONS WITH CITY OFFICIALS TASKED WITH SUBJECTING HIM TO REGULATION, CORRUPTION IS A CONSTANT TEMPTATION. CONTRACTORS HAVE TIES TO ORGANIZED CRIME.

TO BE A PLAYER, YOU MUST BE WILLING TO MAKE COMMITMENTS, SIGN CONTRACTS, KNOW-ING THAT SOME PROMISES ARE MEANT TO BE BROKEN.

NEW YORK IN THE 1970s AND 1980s WAS A DEEPLY DYSFUNCTIONAL CITY. WHITE FLIGHT, URBAN RIOTS, MUNICIPAL BANKRUPTCY, AND HIGH STREET CRIME RATES LEFT THE FIVE BOROUGHS SCARRED WITH ABANDONED BUILDINGS AND EMPTY LOTS. MANY OTHER URBAN CORES HAD SIMILAR PROBLEMS. NATURE ABHORS A VACUUM. WHERE OTHERS SAW RUIN, THE TRUMPS SAW OPPORTUNITY.

SOON AFTER ARRIVING AT WHARTON, DONALD BECAME A "FLIPPER," INVESTING $2 MILLION HE BORROWED FROM HIS FATHER INTO PROPERTIES IN PHILADELPHIA. (THAT'S THE EQUIVALENT OF OVER $13 MILLION TODAY.)

I WOULD FIX UP HOUSES, FIX UP LITTLE BUILDINGS. FIX THEM UP AND SELL THEM, RENT THEM AND LIVE IN THEM... MADE A LITTLE MONEY IN COLLEGE.

NOT MUCH IS KNOWN ABOUT TRUMP'S EARLY FORAYS INTO REAL ESTATE. HE SAYS HIS FATHER WAS PLEASED.

TRUMP TRAVELED HOME TO NEW YORK
EVERY WEEKEND, SOMETIMES GROUSING TO
FRIENDS THAT HIS FATHER WORKED HIM TOO
HARD. FRED'S COMPANY, THEN CALLED
ELIZABETH TRUMP AND SON (SOON RENAMED
THE TRUMP ORGANIZATION AT DONALD'S
BEHEST), SENT DONALD TO TRY TO HELP
SAVE A TROUBLED DEAL IN THE INDUSTRIAL
MIDWEST.

IN 1962, FRED HAD PAID $5.7 MILLION FOR
SWIFTON VILLAGE, A FORECLOSED
APARTMENT COMPLEX IN CINCINNATI. A
$500,000 INVESTMENT HELPED INCREASE
THE OCCUPANCY RATE.

IT WAS MY FIRST
MULTIMILLION
DOLLAR DEAL.

ACTUALLY, FRED MADE HIS SON LEARN THE BUSINESS FROM THE BOTTOM UP.

IN CINCINNATI, THIS HAD MEANT DONALD HAD GOTTEN HIS HANDS DIRTY, IN CHARGE OF THE LANDSCAPING. THAT WAS THE EASY PART.

HIS FATHER HAD A MESS TO CLEAN UP WHEN AN UNDERCOVER HOUSING INVESTIGATOR CALLED OUT THE TRUMP BUSINESS FOR REFUSING TO RENT TO BLACKS. FROM A FINANCIAL STANDPOINT, THE SWIFTON DEAL WAS A MODEST SUCCESS. FRED TRUMP SOLD IT FOR $6.75 MILLION TEN YEARS LATER, IN 1972 -- A RATE OF RETURN LESS THAN HALF OF THE AVERAGE AMERICAN HOME DURING THAT PERIOD.

DONALD'S BIG CONTRIBUTION TO HIS DAD'S BUSINESS WAS TO SELL HIM ON THE JOYS OF LEVERAGING DEBT. AT WHARTON, DONALD HAD BEEN IMPRESSED WITH HOW CREATIVE FINANCING COULD BE USED TO INCREASE LIQUIDITY AND MINIMIZE RISK. OPM -- OTHER PEOPLE'S MONEY -- WAS THE KEY TO GETTING BIG FAST. GOING OVER THE BOOKS, DONALD NOTICED THAT FRED'S RELUCTANCE TO BORROW MONEY HAD LEFT TENS OF MILLIONS IN UNTAPPED EQUITY LOCKED IN HIS BUILDINGS.

IRONICALLY FOR A BUSINESSMAN WHO PROMISES TO RUN THE GOVERNMENT LIKE A CORPORATION, TRUMP HAS LONG BELIEVED THAT THE FEDERAL GOVERNMENT -- UNLIKE THE TRUMP ORGANIZATION -- SHOULD BE DEBT-FREE.

(POLITIFACT RANKED TRUMP'S EIGHT-YEAR PROMISE AS ONE OF THE BIGGEST POLITICAL LIES EVER.) MAYBE HE'S STILL GOT SOME OF THE OLD MAN IN HIM.

BY 1971, DONALD HAD CONVINCED HIS FATHER TO LET HIM TAKE CHARGE OF THE TRUMP ORGANIZATION AS PRESIDENT.

HE HIT THE GROUND RUNNING, WHEELING AND DEALING. HE WAS REALLY INTERESTED IN DISTRESSED PROPERTIES. WHEN THE PENNSYLVANIA CENTRAL RAILROAD WENT BANKRUPT, HE BOUGHT AN OPTION ON THE COMPANY'S RAIL YARDS ON MANHATTAN'S FAR WEST SIDE. BECAUSE THE ECONOMY WAS AWFUL, HE SCRAPPED HIS PLAN TO BUILD LUXURY APARTMENT TOWERS THERE. IN 1978, THE CITY SELECTED THE SITE FOR THE FUTURE JAVITS CONVENTION CENTER. (TRUMP HAD OFFERED TO WAIVE HIS FEE IF THE FACILITY WAS NAMED AFTER HIM.)

half of the Trump deal, which ha ended to increase Penn Central's s land price as well as the size of its the development project. Trump h: ended the contract to provide tha re not allowed to share in th ofits—as the guidelines indicated he t—then he could walk away from th e only loser would be Penn Central, uld then forfeit the $750,000 it woul vanced to cover the developer's p ry expenses.

Getzoff was stunned. But even m cative of Berger's new attitude was oach to Getzoff and a housing con ho had accompanied him to Phila at morning. Getzoff wrote a memo himself immediately after these ev ads: "Mr. Berger took us aside ar sted that 'instead of fighting,' wor ithdraw the HRH proposal so the atter could be settled at the hearir rger stated that he was 'sure tha ayed ball, he could work out a very s ry brokerage commission' for us. e [Getzoff and his consultant] in r. Berger that 'we don't play that me.'"

Getzoff also recalled that later th rump approached him with a simila on: "This arrogant young man pat h the back in a most patronizing i d asked me if I might be his broke red him that I was not in the need g a patron builder. He said that i at you people—meaning brokers—a t."

"I don't think I said that. If I did rump said to me.

I also talked with Edward Rube ow a member of another Philadelp m, who confirmed Getzoff's accour onversation with Berger. "I do recall tle distressed at what happened sked if he could explain the Berger s

GLITZ AND PIZZAZZ WERE JUST AS CENTRAL TO TRUMP'S BUSINESS MODEL AS DEALMAKING. HE SQUIRED ACTRESSES AND STEWARDESSES TO PRICEY MANHATTAN NIGHTCLUBS LIKE THE 21 CLUB, EL MOROCCO, REGINE'S, AND DOUBLES.

IF A MAN HAS **FLAIR**... AND IS SMART AND SOMEWHAT CONSERVATIVE AND HAS A TASTE FOR WHAT PEOPLE WANT, HE'S BOUND TO BE SUCCESSFUL IN NEW YORK.

HE HAD THE SAME ATTITUDE ABOUT ARCHITECTURE. "SLEEK." "MODERN." THOSE WERE ALWAYS WHAT HE WANTED IN HIS BUILDINGS.

SLEEK!

MODERN!

TRUMP DIDN'T MENTION ANOTHER TRAIT HE RELIED UPON: RUTHLESSNESS.

IN OCTOBER 1973, NIXON'S JUSTICE DEPARTMENT FILED A MAJOR LAWSUIT AGAINST THE TRUMP ORGANIZATION FOR HOUSING DISCRIMINATION, SPECIFICALLY FOR REFUSING TO RENT APARTMENTS TO TENANTS OF COLOR AT 39 OF ITS PROPERTIES IN NEW YORK.

THE ACCUSATION THAT HE WAS RACIST WOULD CONTINUE TO DOG HIM THROUGHOUT HIS BUSINESS CAREER AND INTO HIS PRESIDENTIAL CAMPAIGN.

FACED WITH EXPLOSIVE CHARGES, TRUMP HIRED
THE MOST NOTORIOUS ATTORNEY OF THE
20TH CENTURY TO DEFEND HIM -- ROY COHN,
INFAMOUS AS JOE McCARTHY'S SIDEKICK
DURING THE 1950s RED SCARE -- AND
COUNTERSUED. HE ACCUSED THE GOVERNMENT
OF TRYING TO FORCE HIM TO RENT TO
WELFARE RECIPIENTS.

COHN

NICE TRY. IN THE END, THE TRUMPS WERE
FORCED TO SETTLE AND SUBMIT TO REGULAR
MONITORING BY THE URBAN LEAGUE.

TO BE INVOLVED IN THE CONSTRUCTION AND CASINO BUSINESSES IN THE 1970s AND 1980s REQUIRED CONTACT WITH THE MAFIA, WHICH FAMOUSLY CONTROLLED THE CONCRETE BUSINESS. BUT TRUMP MAY HAVE GONE FURTHER THAN HE NEEDED TO JUST TO KEEP THINGS MOVING SMOOTHLY.

COHN, TRUMP'S LAWYER, ALSO REPRESENTED GENOVESE CRIME FAMILY BOSS TONY SALERNO. TRUMP ALSO PALLED AROUND WITH JOHN GOTTI'S ASSOCIATE ROBERT LiBUTTI. THE TRUMP ORGANIZATION BOUGHT LiBUTTI NINE LUXURY CARS.

IN ANOTHER EXAMPLE OF THE TRUMP ORGANIZATION BEING SINGLED OUT FOR ITS RACIST PRACTICES, TRUMP PLAZA CASINO WAS FINED $200,000 FOR AGREEING TO KEEP BLACK GAMBLERS AWAY FROM LiBUTTI'S TABLE.

IN 1981, TRUMP PAID $13 MILLION FOR 100 CENTRAL PARK SOUTH, A HIGH-RISE CALLED BARBIZON PLAZA THAT FACED THE FAMOUS MANHATTAN PARK. THE HIGH-RISE WAS CHEAP BECAUSE THE EXISTING TENANTS HAD BEEN THERE FOR A LONG TIME AND PAID RENTS THAT WERE BY THEN FAR BELOW MARKET.

FOR EXAMPLE, MADELYN RUBINSTEIN PAID $93.08 A MONTH FOR HER RENT-CONTROLLED APARTMENT -- THE SAME PRICE HER GRAND-MOTHER HAD PAID SINCE 1967. THERE WERE THREE-ROOM APARTMENTS FACING CENTRAL PARK WITH RENTS AS LOW AS $436 PER MONTH.

TRUMP COULDN'T EVICT HIS TENANTS LEGALLY. AND HE WAS TOO CHEAP TO BUY THEM OUT.

THE TRUMP ORGANIZATION ORDERED THE BUILDING'S SUPERINTENDENT NOT TO ACCEPT TENANTS' PACKAGES. REPAIRS CEASED.

MUSHROOMS GREW ON THE CARPET IN APARTMENT 14B AS WATER FROM A LEAKY PIPE FILLED THE UNIT.

IT FELT LIKE WE WERE **UNDER ATTACK**. TRUMP DID HIS BEST NOT TO REPAIR ANYTHING.

THAT'S WHEN THINGS TURNED *REALLY* UGLY.

A FIRM BELIEVER THAT THE BEST DEFENSE IS AN OVER-THE-TOP OFFENSE, TRUMP SUED THE TENANTS' LAWYER. THEN, TO TERRORIZE THE REMAINING TENANTS INTO MOVING OUT, TRUMP TOOK OUT ADS IN NEWSPAPERS OFFERING EMPTY UNITS IN THE BUILDING TO HOMELESS PEOPLE. HE EVEN OFFERED TO SUPPLY NURSES AND MEDICAL SUPPLIES.

SOME PEOPLE THINK I'M JUST DOING A NUMBER ON THE PEOPLE IN THE BUILDING. THAT'S NOT TRUE. I JUST WANT TO HELP WITH THE HOMELESS PROBLEM.

CCESS
Sweet It Is
Who Take Risks
Make Millions

News & Culture

Donald Trump Gets What He Wants
Looks for Hot Times

EVERYONE KNEW THE TRUTH: HE WAS WILLING TO DO ANYTHING TO FORCE HIS TENANTS TO MOVE.

AFTER FIVE YEARS OF SHOCK AND AWE, TRUMP LOST HIS BATTLE TO DEMOLISH THE BUILDING. THE REMAINING TENANTS WERE ALLOWED TO STAY. TRUMP PAID THEM AN UNDISCLOSED AMOUNT. NEW YORKERS WHO FOLLOWED THE STORY WERE DISGUSTED.

THIS WAS A CONCRETE CHOICE HE MADE, KNOWING HE WOULD DISRUPT THE LIVES OF MANY MIDDLE INCOME, ELDERLY PEOPLE.

IN THE LATE 1990s, TRUMP CONVERTED THE NON-RENTED UNITS TO CONDOMINIUMS. IN KEEPING WITH HIS PRACTICE OF SLAPPING HIS NAME ON EVERYTHING HE COULD, THE BARBIZON WAS RENAMED THE TRUMP PARC (NOW TRUMP PARC EAST).

WAYNE BARRETT, INVESTIGATIVE REPORTER

David Rozenholc, 100 CPS tenant attorney:

HE KNOWS HOW TO NEGOTIATE, HE KNOWS HOW TO USE LEVERAGE AND HE'S VERY PERCEPTIVE ABOUT HIS OPPONENT'S VULNERABILITIES. IT DIDN'T WORK AGAINST ME, BUT WHEN YOU DEAL WITH PUTIN AND IRAN, THESE COULD BE USEFUL QUALITIES.

RUBINSTEIN, THE RENT-CONTROLLED TENANT, DECIDED INSTEAD TO PAY A DISCOUNTED PRICE OF $150,000 FOR AN APARTMENT NOW WORTH AT LEAST $700,000. SHE WON -- BUT SO DID DONALD. BECAUSE OF NEW YORK'S SOARING REAL ESTATE MARKET IN THE 1980s AND 1990s, TRUMP PARC EAST IS WORTH MANY TIMES WHAT DONALD PAID FOR BARBIZON PLAZA.

BEHIND EVERY FORTUNE IS A CRIME, BALZAC SAID. AS SEEN AT CENTRAL PARK SOUTH, TRUMP'S FORTUNE WAS BUILT ON A WHOLE PATTERN OF SCUZZY BEHAVIOR.

IN 1980, TRUMP HIRED ILLEGAL IMMIGRANTS FROM POLAND TO DEMOLISH THE OLD BONWIT TELLER STORE ON THE SITE WHERE HE PLANNED TO PUT UP TRUMP TOWER. HE PAID THEM SLAVE WAGES: $5 AN HOUR, WHICH THEY DIDN'T ALWAYS RECEIVE. THEY WERE SO POOR THEY SLEPT ON-SITE. THOSE WHO COMPLAINED WERE THREATENED WITH DEPORTATION.

Wojciech Kozak:

WE WORKED IN HORRID, TERRIBLE CONDITIONS. WE WERE FRIGHTENED ILLEGAL IMMIGRANTS AND DIDN'T KNOW ENOUGH ABOUT OUR RIGHTS.

THE WORKERS SUED AND EVENTUALLY WON IN COURT.

TRUMP WAS AN EQUAL OPPORTUNITY ASSHOLE. HE SCREWED OVER BANKERS AT LEAST AS OFTEN AS IMPOVERISHED DAY LABORERS. I WAS NEARLY ONE OF THEM.

IN THE LATE 1980s, I WAS A LOAN OFFICER AT THE INDUSTRIAL BANK OF JAPAN'S NEW YORK OFFICE. MY BOSS ASKED ME TO CRUNCH THE NUMBERS ON TRUMP'S LOAN APPLICATION FOR HIS TRUMP TAJ MAHAL CASINO IN ATLANTIC CITY.

IT WASN'T A HARD CALL.

MY BOSS RELUCTANTLY FOLLOWED MY
RECOMMENDATION THAT WE NOT GET
INVOLVED.

OTHER BANKS FUNDED THE TAJ USING HIGH-
INTEREST JUNK BONDS. THEY GOT HOSED.
TRUMP TOOK THE TAJ INTO BANKRUPTCY.
(MY BOSS WAS PLEASED.) TRUMP'S CASINO
OPERATIONS HAVE GONE INTO CHAPTER 11
BANKRUPTCY FOUR TIMES OVER THE YEARS.
TRUMP'S POSTURE IS, IF YOU'RE STUPID
ENOUGH TO BELIEVE HIS SALES PITCH, YOU
DESERVE WHAT YOU GET. AS FAR AS HE'S
CONCERNED, THERE'S NOTHING DISHONORABLE
ABOUT BEING A DEADBEAT.

IN 2016, AFTER TRUMP ANNOUNCED THAT HE WOULD BE IGNORING THE TRADITION THAT PRESIDENTIAL CANDIDATES RELEASE THEIR TAX RETURNS, MITT ROMNEY (ANOTHER BILLIONAIRE) SPECULATED WHY:

I THINK WE HAVE GOOD REASON TO BELIEVE THAT THERE'S A **BOMBSHELL** IN DONALD TRUMP'S TAXES. EITHER HE'S NOT ANYWHERE AS WEALTHY AS HE SAYS HE IS, OR HE HASN'T BEEN PAYING THE KIND OF TAXES WE WOULD EXPECT HIM TO PAY.

LIKE OTHER "WEALTHY" PEOPLE BUT TO AN EXTREME, TRUMP CREATED THE ILLUSION THAT HE WAS RICHER THAN HE REALLY WAS. MAINLY HE DID THIS BY LEASING HIS NAME TO BUILDINGS HE DOESN'T OWN. TRUMP CITY, A SERIES OF LUXURY HIGH-RISES BEARING THE TRUMP NAME IN THE WEST 60s IN MANHATTAN, IS ACTUALLY OWNED BY A HONG KONG INVESTMENT FIRM.

THERE ARE 17 BUILDINGS NAMED "TRUMP" IN MANHATTAN -- TRUMP SOHO, TRUMP PLAZA, TRUMP WORLD TOWER, ETC. -- BUT HE ONLY OWNS A HANDFUL OF THEM.

YET, IN OUR ECONOMY WHERE MONEY IS MOSTLY MADE THROUGH FINANCIAL ALGORITHMS AND BRANDING, NOT MAKING THINGS, TRUMP'S HOLLOW FORTUNE HAS BECOME A REAL ONE. EVEN IF HE ISN'T WORTH AS MUCH AS HE SAYS HE IS, HE'S STILL ONE OF THE RICHEST MEN IN THE U.S. TRUMP SAYS HIS NET WORTH IS $10 BILLION. EXPERTS BELIEVE THE FIGURE IS CLOSER TO $4.1 BILLION. (TRUMP INCLUDES HIS PERSONAL SELF-ASSESSMENT OF HIS NAME'S "BRAND VALUE" IN HIS STATEMENTS OF NET WORTH.)

IT'S THE AMERICAN WAY: FAKE IT UNTIL YOU MAKE IT. IT'S BEEN A LONG JOURNEY, BUT DONALD TRUMP FINALLY APPEARS TO HAVE MADE IT.

NET WORTH OF 2016 PRESIDENTIAL CANDIDATES:

DONALD TRUMP (R):
$4.1 BILLION

TEXAS SENATOR TED CRUZ (R):
$3 MILLION

OHIO GOVERNOR JOHN KASICH (R):
$2.5 MILLION

FORMER PRESIDENT BILL AND FORMER SECRETARY OF STATE HILLARY CLINTON (D):
$111 MILLION

VERMONT SENATOR BERNIE SANDERS (I):
$436,000

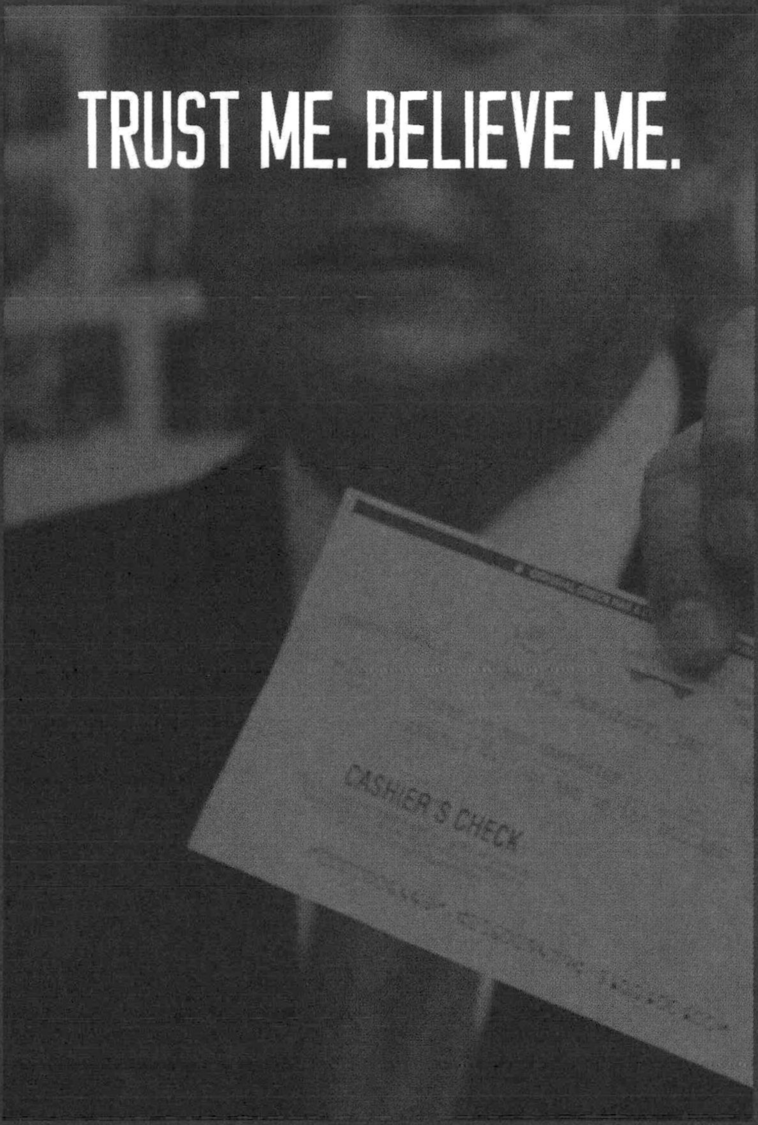
TRUST ME. BELIEVE ME.
CASHIER'S CHECK

IN RECENT YEARS, ANTI-IMMIGRATION REPUBLICANS RELIED ON "DOG WHISTLES" -- CAREFULLY CODED MESSAGES WHOSE MEANING WAS UNDERSTOOD BUT COULD BE PLAUSIBLY DENIED -- TO APPEAL TO RIGHT-WING VOTERS WITHOUT OPENLY EMBRACING THEM.

TO APPEAL TO RACIST REPUBLICANS, RONALD REAGAN LAUNCHED HIS 1980 CAMPAIGN IN THE MISSISSIPPI TOWN WHERE THREE FREEDOM RIDERS WERE MURDERED BY THE KLAN IN 1964, TALKING ABOUT "STATES' RIGHTS" -- A PHRASE USED TO JUSTIFY SEGREGATION.

RIGHT OUT OF THE GATE, TRUMP SHOWED HE HAD NO SCRUPLES. HE'D SAY OR DO WHATEVER IT TOOK TO WIN, EVEN IF IT MEANT PLAYING POLITICAL FOOTSY WITH THE SCUM OF THE EARTH. WHEN FORMER KKK GRAND WIZARD DAVID DUKE ENDORSED HIM -- AS DID MANY ON THE EXTREME FRINGES OF THE FAR RIGHT -- HE PLAYED CUTE, REFUSING TO DIS HIM.

I DON'T KNOW ANYTHING ABOUT WHAT YOU'RE EVEN TALKING ABOUT WITH WHITE SUPREMACY OR WHITE SUPREMACISTS. SO I DON'T KNOW. I DON'T KNOW— DID HE ENDORSE ME, OR WHAT'S GOING ON?

DAVID DUKE

TOM METZGER, White Aryan Resistance founder

DON BLACK, Stormfront Aryan-power website

UNDER A TRUMP PRESIDENCY, THE POLITICS OF RACE AND IMMIGRATION WOULD MOVE FAR RIGHT.

RACISTS LIKE DUKE AND WHITE-POWER ORGANIZATIONS COULD BECOME LEGITIMIZED, PERHAPS EVEN MAINSTREAMED. AND HIS POLITICS -- THROWING OUT UNDOCUMENTED MEXICANS, POLICE REGISTRIES FOR MUSLIMS -- THOSE ARE THEIR POLITICS TOO.

CONSIDERING HOW EXTREME SOME OF THE THINGS TRUMP SAID REALLY WERE, REACTIONS TO TRUMP'S RANTS WERE REMARKABLY TEPID, EVEN IN THE MEDIA.

EDITORIAL WRITERS AND DEMOCRATS ISSUED DUTIFUL CONDEMNATIONS OF TRUMP'S OUTRAGEOUS RHETORIC. BUT FEW OF THEM TOOK HIM, OR HIS CHANCES OF BECOMING PRESIDENT, SERIOUSLY ENOUGH.

Ross Douthat, New York Times

Dec. 26, 2015

"Now: Trump will not be the Republican nominee (yes, really)."

AS THE REPUBLICAN PRIMARY PROCESS BEGAN
TO WIND DOWN, TRUMP BEGAN ASSUMING A
MORE MODERATE TONE IN HIS PUBLIC
APPEARANCES.

HE HIRED PROFESSIONAL POLITICAL ADVISORS.
HE READ FROM NOTECARDS. DETERMINED TO
PROTECT HIS LEAD SO HE COULD GO TO THE
REPUBLICAN CONVENTION WITH THE 1,237
DELEGATES NECESSARY TO WIN ON THE FIRST
BALLOT, HE DECIDED TO ACT "PRESIDENTIAL."

Trump's wife and daughter 'beg' him
to act more presidential

Donald Trump goes for a more presidential
tone — for now

Donald Trump Says Ivanka and Melania 'Begged'
Him to Act More Presidential – but He Doesn't
Want To

**Donald Trump's campaign
says he's going to act more
presidential**

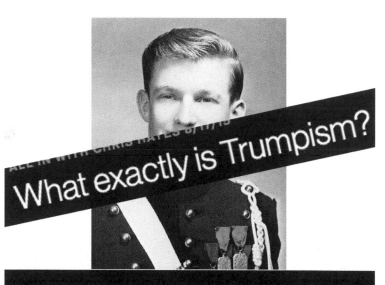

What exactly is Trumpism?

A SMART BUT LAZY STUDENT WHO LIKED TO CUT CORNERS, TRUMP CRAMMED FOR THE PRIMARIES LIKE HE DID AT WHARTON THE NIGHT BEFORE A FINAL EXAM. HE TOOK IN POLICY BRIEFINGS AND READ WHITE PAPERS.

ONCE IT BECAME CLEAR THAT HE WAS GOING TO WIN THE REPUBLICAN PRESIDENTIAL NOMINATION -- THOUGH, DUE TO HIS RELUCTANCE TO STUDY THE DETAILS, RIVAL TED CRUZ HAD MANAGED TO WORK THE PROCESS TO PEEL AWAY SOME OF THE DELEGATES IN STATES TRUMP HAD WON -- HE WORKED TO FIGURE OUT REALLY, TRULY, WHAT HE BELIEVED IN.

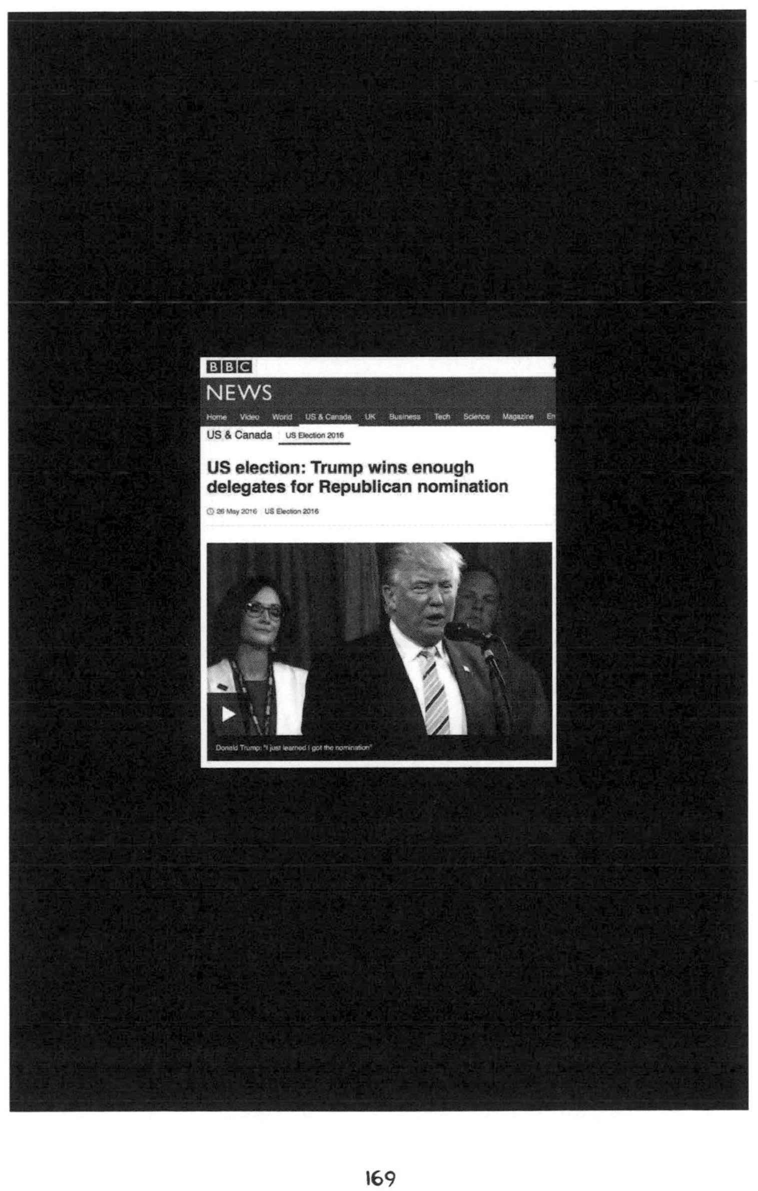
BBC

NEWS

Home Video World US & Canada UK Business Tech Science Magazine En

US & Canada US Election 2016

US election: Trump wins enough delegates for Republican nomination

26 May 2016 US Election 2016

Donald Trump: "I just learned I got the nomination"

AFTER EIGHT YEARS OF THE CAREFULLY
SCRIPTED BARACK OBAMA, A BIG PART OF
TRUMP'S APPEAL MIGHT BE JUST HOW
DIFFERENT HE IS FROM WHAT PRECEDED HIM.

BUT MY SPECIFICS ARE
VERY— I'M GOING TO
GET GREAT PEOPLE THAT
KNOW WHAT THEY'RE
DOING, NOT A BUNCH OF
POLITICAL HACKS THAT
HAVE NO IDEA... APPOINTED
BY PRESIDENT OBAMA,
THAT DOESN'T HAVE A CLUE.

AT A TIME WHEN GOVERNMENT MAY BE DOING LESS TO HELP PEOPLE IN NEED THAN IT HAS IN OVER A CENTURY, IT'S TEMPTING TO LISTEN TO A STRONG-WILLED LEADER WHO SAYS HE CAN GET THINGS DONE THROUGH NAKED FORCE AND POWER OF PERSONALITY.

THEY WON'T REFUSE. THEY'RE NOT GOING TO REFUSE ME, BELIEVE ME. IF I SAY DO IT, THEY'RE GOING TO DO IT, THAT'S WHAT LEADERSHIP IS ALL ABOUT.

DonaldJTrump.com

TR

mp.com

TRUMP

ACTUALLY, IN A DEMOCRACY, LEADERSHIP IS ABOUT PERSUASION, NOT ORDERING, NOR AWING VIA CHARISMA, NOR RULING BY FEAR.

IT'S EASY TO IMAGINE THE BUSINESS TYCOON SEIZING CONTROL OF THE FEDERAL BUDGET FROM A FECKLESS CONGRESS.

TRUMPISM WOULD LOOK LIKE PUTINISM IN RUSSIA: AUTHORITARIAN RULE WITH THE TRAPPINGS OF DEMOCRACY. CONTROL OVER SPENDING WOULD LET TRUMP GET THINGS DONE THAT HAVE LONG BEEN OVERDUE.

NO MORE GOVERNMENT SHUTDOWNS! NO MORE CLOSED NATIONAL PARKS! I'VE BEEN BALANCING BUDGETS FOR YEARS, SO LEAVE THIS TO **ME**.

HIGH-SPEED "TRUMP RAIL" OPENS IN 2019.

BECAUSE ILLEGAL IMMIGRANTS WERE THE INITIAL JUSTIFICATION FOR HIS CAMPAIGN, TRUMP WOULD HAVE TO FOLLOW THROUGH ON HIS PROMISE TO DEPORT MILLIONS OF THEM.

IT WOULD BE HORRIFIC. FOR THOSE WHO REMAIN BEHIND, HOWEVER, (LOW-PAYING) JOBS WOULD BE MORE PLENTIFUL.

TROUBLE, IN ANY CASE, WOULD BE HARD-WIRED INTO A TRUMP ADMINISTRATION. SOONER OR LATER, A TYRANT'S THOUGHTS TURN TO TARGETING ENEMIES -- HIS ENEMIES, THE ENEMIES OF HIS ALLIES, ENEMIES OF THE STATE.

"Democracy is beautiful in theory; in practice it is a fallacy. You in America will see that some day."

—*Attributed to Benito Mussolini*

Afterword

Many Americans are asking themselves how Donald Trump managed to win the Republican nomination for president. The answer is, of course, simple: more people voted for him than for Jeb Bush, Marco Rubio, Ted Cruz, and his other opponents in the primaries. But why? How is it possible, his detractors ask, that a man with no experience as an elected official, a caustic personality with a long history of controversies, who seems more interested in acquiring enemies than allies, has a chance of being elected president of the United States? What is so special about this man, so unconcerned with decorum that he appeared on WWE, that allowed him to convince the media to give him, by one estimate, $2 billion in free media coverage?

What is the source of Trump's unique charisma? How did he convince tens of millions of voters to choose him?

Those are valid things to wonder about. You may have picked up this book in search of answers to those questions. But I don't think that they are the most important concerns we ought to be addressing.

The wild 2016 election season says more about

us and the American system of electoral politics than it does about Donald Trump, Hillary Clinton, Bernie Sanders, or the nearly two dozen other contenders who fell by the wayside. This is about more than whether Donald Trump is really a racist or whether Hillary Clinton is truly dishonest. This is about the failure of the two-party system, touted to schoolchildren as the best political system ever created by mankind, to address citizens' most basic needs.

There's still lots of lingering pain from the 2007-2008 economic crisis. Americans feel more hopeless about the future then at any time in recent memory. They suspect that this time, America really *is* in decline and there's *never* going to be any coming back. On the Democratic side, Bernie Sanders addressed the concerns of the downwardly mobile by arguing that traditional liberalism could recreate the social safety net. Among Republicans, only Donald Trump offered something new, albeit vague: the assertion that it was still possible to "make America great again."

It probably isn't possible to make America great again, not in the way that people think. Jobs that were exported overseas are probably never coming back. Salaries will probably never rise as quickly as they did during the boom that followed World War II. What's notable about Trump's campaign slogan, especially since it comes from the right, is the *acknowledgment* that things are not great. That people are suffering. For a long time, the political class has pretended everything is fine, that nothing has changed. Poverty? That is something that happens overseas, not here.

Tens of millions of people have been willing to overlook Trump's flaws as a candidate and as a human being because of that acknowledgment. Jimmy Carter, it seems, was ahead of his time when he warned that we were in danger of succumbing to *malaise*. (I know, he didn't use that exact word. But still.)

What if, as seems likely, Trump is nothing more than a charlatan? If he wins the presidency, we are about to embark on a remarkable experiment. Can a person with nominal party affiliation and support govern effectively? Separately, will we see a democratically elected president transform our country into an authoritarian, or even fascist, state? Alternatively, is it possible that Donald Trump will turn out to be something long promised but that we no longer expect to see: the brilliant CEO who saves the economy and political system by running the country like a business?

No one knows what he'll do.

He doesn't know what he'll do.

Which is why he could win.

Notes

8   Images: http://photos1.blogger.com/blogger/2398/858/1600/
        DSC04481.jpg; http://www.coalcampusa.com/rustbelt/oh/
        frigidaire.jpg\; https://s-media-cache-ak0.pinimg.com/736x/32/05/
        61/320561566199b7ee86ce5da206350cc7.jpg.

10   Tanvi Misra, "Where Minority Populations Have Become the Majority,"
        CityLab, April 9, 2015, http://www.citylab.com/housing/2015/04/where-
        minority-populations-have-become-the-majority/390126.
        Julia Preston, "Pink Slips at Disney. But First, Training Foreign Replacements,"
        New York Times, June 3, 2015, http://www.nytimes.com/2015/06/04/us/last-
        task-after-layoff-at-disney-train-foreign-replacements.html.

11   http://www.doctorhousingbubble.com/wp-content/uploads/2010/05/1-
        homes-in-foreclosure.jpg.

12   In 2009, just 53% of Americans told pollsters they thought that
        capitalism was a better system than socialism or communism. "Just 53%
        Say Capitalism Better Than Socialism," Rasmussen Reports, April 9, 2009,
        http://www.rasmussenreports.com/public_content/politics/general_
        politics/april_2009/just_53_say_capitalism_better_than_socialism.

14   Eric Weiner, "Subprime Bailout: Good Idea or 'Moral Hazard?,'" WBUR,
        November 29, 2007, http://www.wbur.org/npr/16734629.

15   Eyder Peralta, "Report: Fed Committed $7.77 Trillion To Rescue Banks,"
        NPR.org, November 28, 2011, http://www.npr.org/sections/thetwo-
        way/2011/11/28/142854391/report-fed-committed-7-77-trillion-to-
        rescue-banks.

19   Mark Murray, "The Tea Party, Four Years Later," NBC News, April 16,
        2013, http://firstread.nbcnews.com/_news/2013/04/16/17780916-the-
        tea-party-four-years-later.

20   Mother Mags, "How Many Inmates Have Died in Sheriff Joe Arpaio's Jail?
        Who Knows, But It's a Big Number," AlterNet.org, December 4, 2015,
        http://www.alternet.org/civil-liberties/how-many-inmates-have-died-
        sheriff-joe-arpaios-jails-who-knows-its-big-number.
            Jens Manual Krogstad and Mark Hugo Lopez, "5 Takeaways About
        the 2014 Latino Vote," Pew Research Center, November 10, 2014, http://
        www.pewresearch.org/fact-tank/2014/11/10/5-takeaways-about-the-
        2014-latino-vote.
            Photo: http://pvangels.com/news-mexico/images/201206/us-deported.jpg.

21   http://www.cnn.com/2014/04/24/politics/bush-clinton-political-dynasties;
      http://www.theguardian.com/us-news/2015/jun/16/hillary-clinton-jeb-
      bush-political-dynasties-voters-candidates; http://www.telegraph.co.uk/
      news/worldnews/us-politics/11669177/America-deserves-better-than-
      Clinton-v-Bush.html.

22   Jeffrey M. Jones, "Economy Trumps Foreign Affairs as Key 2016 Election
      Issue," Gallup, May 15, 2015, http://www.gallup.com/poll/183164/
      economy-trumps-foreign-affairs-key-2016-election-issue.aspx.

      Gabriel Fisher, "Trickle Down Economics Is Wrong, Says IMF,"
      Quartz, June 16, 2015, http://qz.com/429487/a-new-imf-study-debunks-
      trickle-down-economics/.

      Celeste Katz, "Jeb Bush Shares Plans to Lower Income Tax in
      Economic Policy Speech, Jabs Hillary Clinton and Donald Trump," New
      York Daily News, September 9, 2015, http://www.nydailynews.com/
      news/politics/jeb-bush-reveals-tax-plans-economic-policy-speech-
      article-1.2354113.

      Steve Peoples, "John Kasich Unveils Tax Plan, Vows to Balance
      Budget Within Eight Years," Huffington Post, October 15, 2015,
      http://www.huffingtonpost.com/entry/john-kasich-tax-plan_
      us_561fce63e4b028dd7ea6ee15.

23   Lloyd Green, "Trump in Phoenix: Mexicans Are Coming to Take Your
      Jobs and Kill You," Daily Beast, July 11, 2015, http://www.thedailybeast.
      com/articles/2015/07/11/trump-in-phoenix-mexicans-are-coming-to-
      take-your-jobs-and-kill-you.html.

24   Lloyd Green, "Trump in Phoenix."

26   "Pat Buchanan on Immigration," OnTheIssues.org, http://www.
      ontheissues.org/Celeb/Pat_Buchanan_Immigration.htm.

27   Anna Brand, "Donald Trump: I Would Force Mexico to Build Border
      Wall," MSNBC, June 28, 2015, http://www.msnbc.com/msnbc/donald-
      trump-i-would-force-mexico-build-border-wall.

      Fred Imbert, "Donald Trump: Mexico Going to Pay for Wall," CNBC,
      October 28, 2015, http://www.cnbc.com/2015/10/28/donald-trump-
      mexico-going-to-pay-for-wall.html.

28   "Forced Population Transfers," GlobalSecurity.org, http://www.
      globalsecurity.org/military/world/war/forced-population-transfers.htm.

      Images: http://cyprus-mail.com/wp-content/uploads/bfi_thumb/Mein-
      Kampf-69jia2lus62yyxqhn8eoq97gialgnndpyeow4bb4k5a.jpg; https://
      redyouthuk.files.wordpress.com/2016/02/joseph-stalin.jpeg.

29   Donald Trump Wants to Deport Every Single Illegal Immigrant—Could
      He?," BBC, November 11, 2015, http://www.bbc.com/news/world-us-
      canada-34789502.

      Lauren Fox, "Donald Trump Wants to Use a "Deportation Force"
      to Remove 11 Million Immigrants From the U.S.," Atlantic, November
      11, 2015, http://www.theatlantic.com/politics/archive/2015/11/donald-

trump-wants-to-use-a-deportation-force-to-remove-11-million-immigrants-from-the-us/445917.

30 Charlie Hebdo Attack: Three Days of Terror," BBC, January 14, 2015, http://www.bbc.com/news/world-europe-30708237/.

Stephanie Condon, "Obama Responds to San Bernardino Shooting," CBS News, December 2, 2015, http://www.cbsnews.com/news/obama-responds-to-san-bernardino-shooting.

Karl de Vries, "Barack Obama Calls Paris Massacre 'Outrageous,'" CNN, November 14, 2015, http://www.cnn.com/2015/11/13/politics/paris-terror-attacks-obama.

Images: http://i2.cdn.turner.com/cnnnext/dam/assets/150108183801-paris-bloody-hallway-super-169.jpg; https://d.ibtimes.co.uk/en/full/1470380/abdelhamid-abaaoud-syria.jpg.

31 Jeremy Diamond, "Donald Trump: Ban All Muslim Travel to U.S.," CNN, December 8, 2015, http://www.cnn.com/2015/12/07/politics/donald-trump-muslim-ban-immigration.

Caitlin Cruz, "Trump Camp Contradicts Itself On Whether Muslim Ban Covers US Citizens," *Talking Points Memo*, December 8, 2015, http://talkingpointsmemo.com/dc/does-trumps-muslim-ban-include-citizens.

32 Trip Gabriel, "Donald Trump Says He'd 'Absolutely' Require Muslims to Register," *New York Times*, November 20, 2015, http://www.nytimes.com/politics/first-draft/2015/11/20/donald-trump-says-hed-absolutely-require-muslims-to-register.

Meaghan Keneally, "Donald Trump Cites These FDR Policies to Defend Muslim Ban," ABC News, December 8, 2015, http://abcnews.go.com/Politics/donald-trump-cites-fdr-policies-defend-muslim-ban/story?id=35648128.

33 Scott Pelley, "Trump Gets Down to Business on 60 Minutes," CBS News, September 27, 2015, http://www.cbsnews.com/news/donald-trump-60-minutes-scott-pelley.

34 Adam Davidson, "Do Illegal Immigrants Actually Hurt the U.S. Economy?" *New York Times*, February 12, 2013, http://www.nytimes.com/2013/02/17/magazine/do-illegal-immigrants-actually-hurt-the-us-economy.html.

Michael Greenstone and Adam Looney, "What Immigration Means for U.S. Employment and Wages," Brookings Institution, May 4, 2012, http://www.brookings.edu/blogs/jobs/posts/2012/05/04-jobs-greenstone-looney.

Chart: http://www.brookings.edu/~/media/Research/Files/Blogs/2012/5/04-jobs-greenstone-looney/050412_chart1.png.

Image: http://image.lehighvalleylive.com/home/lvlive-media/width620/img/breaking-news_impact/photo/17336343-mmmain.jpg.

35 Proclamation to the German Nation," EmersonKent.com, http://www.emersonkent.com/speeches/proclamation_to_the_german_nation.htm.

39   http://www.dailymail.co.uk/femail/article-3209079/Ivanka-Trump-s-one-
      year-old-son-Joseph-spitting-image-grandpa-Donald-sweet-Instagram-
      snap-s-mastered-hairstyle.html
         Images: http://www.newsday.com/news/nation/young-donald-trump-
      pictures-1.11583814; https://media2.wnyc.org/i/800/533/l/80/1/TRUMP-
      FAMILY-HOME-IN-JAMAICA-ESTATES.jpg.
40   Peter Geoghegan, "Few Rooting for Donald Trump on His Mother's
      Scottish Island," *Irish Times*, May 28, 2016, http://www.irishtimes.com/
      news/world/us/few-rooting-for-donald-trump-on-his-mother-s-scottish-
      island-1.2663636.
         Images: http://i.dailymail.co.uk/i/pix/2013/01/31/article-2271362-
      17445DBA000005DC-814_634x328.jpg; http://i.bullfax.com/
      imgs/1207a9ae48d66ebd1ecd706dd64a93ad290aadfa.jpg.
41   Tracie Rozhon, "Fred C. Trump, Postwar Master Builder of Housing for
      Middle Class, Dies at 93," *New York Times*, June 26, 1999, http://www.
      nytimes.com/1999/06/26/nyregion/fred-c-trump-postwar-master-builder-
      of-housing-for-middle-class-dies-at-93.html?pagewanted=all.
         Image: https://heavyeditorial.files.wordpress.com/2016/01/fred-
      trump.jpg?quality=65&strip=all&strip=all.
42   Jason Horowitz, "For Donald Trump, Lessons From a Brother's
      Suffering," *New York Times*, January 2, 2016, http://www.nytimes.
      com/2016/01/03/us/politics/for-donald-trump-lessons-from-a-brothers-
      suffering.html.
         'Donald Trump Biography," Biography.com, http://www.biography.
      com/people/donald-trump-9511238#synopsis.
         Matt Viser, "Even in College, Donald Trump Was Brash," *Boston
      Globe*, August 28, 2015, https://www.bostonglobe.com/news/
      nation/2015/08/28/donald-trump-was-bombastic-even-wharton-
      business-school/3FO0j1uS5X6S8156yH3YhL/story.html.
43   Ailsa Chang, "This Is Where Donald Trump Played by the Rules and
      Learned to Beat the Game," NPR.org, November 10, 2015, http://www.
      npr.org/2015/11/10/455331251/this-is-where-donald-trump-played-by-
      the-rules-and-learned-to-beat-the-game.
         Chuck Hadad, "Photos Tell the Story of Donald Trump's Early Years,"
      CNN, April 15, 2016, http://www.cnn.com/2016/04/15/politics/early-
      trump-photos.
45   Chang, "This Is Where Donald Trump Played by the Rules and Learned
      to Beat the Game."
46   Ibid.
         Image: https://img.washingtonpost.com/rw/2010-2019/.
      WashingtonPost/2016/01/09/National-Enterprise/Images/We-want-to-
      use-these-007145236331 1.jpg?uuid=72AV0rb8EeWKvNCTku3GEg
48   Chang, "This Is Where Donald Trump Played by the Rules and Learned
      to Beat the Game."

49   Dan Spinelli, "Trump Flaunts Wharton Degree, But His College Years Remain a Mystery," *Daily Pennsylvanian*, August 19, 2015, http://www.thedp.com/article/2015/08/donald-trump-wharton-classmates.

50   Viser, "Even in College."

53   Ashley Parker, "Donald Trump Frowns on Idea of 'Toning It Down,' Despite Aide's Comments," *New York Times*, April 23, 2016, http://www.nytimes.com/politics/first-draft/2016/04/23/donald-trump-frowns-on-idea-of-toning-it-down-despite-aides-comments.

54   Michael E. Miller, "Donald Trump on a Protester: 'I'd Like to Punch Him in the Face,'" *Washington Post*, February 23, 2016, https://www.washingtonpost.com/news/morning-mix/wp/2016/02/23/donald-trump-on-protester-id-like-to-punch-him-in-the-face/.

       Jonathan Swan, "Trump Tells Security to Take Protesters' Coats: 'Throw Them Out into the Cold,'" *Hill*, January 7, 2016, http://thehill.com/blogs/ballot-box/presidential-races/265172-trump-tells-security-to-confiscate-protesters-coats.

56   Sophie Tatum, "Trump Trashtalk: 7 Attacks The Donald Threw in His Announcement Speech," CNN, June 16, 2015, http://www.cnn.com/2015/06/16/politics/donald-trump-attacks-obama-opponents.

       Patrick J. Buchanan, "What Trump Has Wrought," LewRockwell.com, April 5, 2016, https://www.lewrockwell.com/2016/04/patrick-j-buchanan/trump-wrought.

59   Matthew Boyle, "'Win, Win, Win!': Donald Trump Zones in on Core Populist Nationalist Issues—We'll Makes America 'Greater than Ever Before,'" *Breitbart*, March 13, 2016, http://www.breitbart.com/big-government/2016/03/13/donald-trump-zones-in-on-core-populist-nationalist-issues-well-make-america-greater-than-ever-before.

63   Conor Friedersdorf, "When Donald Trump Became a Celebrity," *Atlantic*, January 6, 2016, http://www.theatlantic.com/politics/archive/2016/01/the-decade-when-donald-trump-became-a-celebrity/422838.

65   Tierney McAfee, "Donald Trump Opens Up About His Brother's Death from Alcoholism: It Had a 'Profound Impact on My Life," *People*, October 8, 2015, http://www.people.com/article/donald-trump-brother-fred-death-alcoholism.

       Image: https://s3-us-west-2.amazonaws.com/find-a-grave-prod/photos/2015/239/105719907_1440788312.jpg.

66   Friedersdorf, "When Donald Trump Became a Celebrity."

67.   Aaron Oster, "Donald Trump and WWE: How the Road to the White House Began at 'WrestleMania,'" *Rolling Stone*, February 1, 2016, http://www.rollingstone.com/sports/features/donald-trump-and-wwe-how-the-road-to-the-white-house-began-at-wrestlemania-20160201#ixzz46apYb4Dh.

       Image: https://maxcdn2.laprogressive.com/wp-content/uploads/2015/09/donald-trump-shaves-720.jpg.

68   "The World's Billionaires," *Forbes*, http://www.forbes.com/profile/donald-trump. Screenshot of http://www.forbes.com/profile/donald-trump/.

Timothy L. O'Brien, "What's He Really Worth?," *New York Times*, October 23, 2005, http://www.nytimes.com/2005/10/23/business/yourmoney/whats-he-really-worth.html.

Claire Groden, "Donald Trump Would Be Richer if He'd Have Invested in Index Funds," *Fortune*, August 20, 2015, http://fortune.com/2015/08/20/donald-trump-index-funds/.

Chase Peterson-Withorn, "How Donald Trump Exagerrates and Fibs About His $4.5 Billion Net Worth," *Forbes*, March 31, 2016, http://www.forbes.com/sites/chasewithorn/2016/03/31/how-donald-trump-exaggerates-and-fibs-about-his-4-5-billion-net-worth.

AJ Agrawal, "TRUMPED: The Donald Has Filed for Bankruptcy Multiple Times. What's His Strategy, and What Can It Teach You?," *Huffington Post*, October 28, 2015, http://www.huffingtonpost.com/aj-agrawal/trumped-the-donald-has-fi_b_8403708.html.

69   Reena Flores, "Donald Trump, Jeb Bush Spar Over Bush Family Legacy," CBS News, February 13, 2016, http://www.cbsnews.com/news/republican-debate-donald-trump-jeb-bush-spar-over-bush-family-legacy.

75   Dana Schuster, "Ivana Trump on How She Advises Donald—And Those Hands," *New York Post*, April 3, 2016, http://nypost.com/2016/04/03/ivana-trump-opens-up-about-how-she-advises-donald-his-hands.

Marie Brenner, "After the Gold Rush," *Vanity Fair*, September 1, 1990, http://www.vanityfair.com/magazine/2015/07/donald-ivana-trump-divorce-prenup-marie-brenner.

76   http://www.dailymail.co.uk/news/article-2385183/Donald-Trumps-ex-wife-Marla-Maples-confesses-loves-him.html.

77   "20 Things You Never Knew About Melania Trump," LifeDaily, http://www.lifedaily.com/20-things-you-never-knew-about-melania-trump/4.

78   Jonathan Van Meter, "Did Their Father Really Know Best?," *New York*, http://nymag.com/nymetro/news/people/features/10610/index4.html.

Jonathan Mahler, "In Campaign and Company, Ivanka Trump Has a Central Role," *New York Times*, April 16, 2016, http://www.nytimes.com/2016/04/17/us/politics/ivanka-trump-donald-trump.html. Image: https://i.ytimg.com/vi/_Otk1FRbNR8/maxresdefault.jpg.

79   Nina Bahadur, "18 Real Things Donald Trump Has Actually Said About Women," *Huffington Post*, August 19, 2015, http://www.huffingtonpost.com/entry/18-real-things-donald-trump-has-said-about-women_us_55d356a8e4b07addcb442023.

Hannah Parry, "Draft Dodger Trump Says Sex in the Eighties Was 'His Personal Vietnam' During Howard Stern Interview in 1997," *Daily Mail*, February 17, 2016, http://www.dailymail.co.uk/news/article-3451452/Trump-says-sex-eighties-personal-Vietnam-Howard-Stern-interview-1997.html.

Seth Millstein, "Donald Trump's Horribly Sexist Criticism of Carly Fiorina During the Debate Is One Every Woman Is Sick of Hearing," *Bustle*, November 10, 2015, http://www.bustle.com/articles/123005-donald-trumps-horribly-sexist-criticism-of-carly-fiorina-during-the-debate-is-one-every-woman-is.

80 Ronald Kessler, "If You Want to Know How Donald Trump Would Run the White House, Take a Look at How He Operates Mar-a-Lago," *Daily Mail*, February 29, 2016, http://www.dailymail.co.uk/news/article-3464605/If-want-know-Donald-Trump-run-White-House-look-operates-Mar-Lago.html.

83 http://www.newsmax.com/Headline/donald-trump-healthcare-no-people-dying/2016/02/06/id/713088/.

"Transcript: Donald Trump Expounds on His Foreign Policy Views," *New York Times*, March 26, 2016, http://www.nytimes.com/2016/03/27/us/politics/donald-trump-transcript.html.

87 David Sherfinski, "Donald Trump: Mitt Romney 'Choked Like a Dog' in 2012," *Washington Times*, November 11, 2015, http://www.washingtontimes.com/news/2015/nov/11/donald-trump-mitt-romney-choked-dog-2012.

Heather Haddon, "Donald Trump's Presidential Run Was Long in the Making," *Wall Street Journal*, March 2, 2016, http://www.wsj.com/articles/donald-trumps-presidential-run-was-long-in-the-making-1456964836.

88 Haddon, "Donald Trump's Presidential Run."

91 Kyle Smith, "Stop Pretending—Donald Trump Is Not Running for President," *New York Post*, May 30, 2015, http://nypost.com/2015/05/30/stop-pretending-donald-trump-is-not-running-for-president.

92 http://www.thedailybeast.com/articles/2016/03/01/trump-used-anti-obama-riffs-against-reagan-first.html.

93 Jeremy Diamond, "Donald Trump Jumps In: The Donald's Latest White House Run Is Officially On," CNN, June 17, 2015, http://www.cnn.com/2015/06/16/politics/donald-trump-2016-announcement-elections/.

94 David Ferguson, "McCain: We'll Make Border with Mexico Look Like 'the Berlin Wall,'" *Raw Story*, June 25, 2013, http://www.rawstory.com/2013/06/mccain-well-make-border-with-mexico-look-like-the-berlin-wall.

David Sherfinski, "Donald Trump: 'Great Wall' on Mexican Border—But Not Canadian Border," *Washington Times*, August 20, 2015, http://www.washingtontimes.com/news/2015/aug/20/donald-trump-great-wall-mexican-border-not-canada.

David Wright, "Vicente Fox Says It Again—This Time on Live TV: 'I'm Not Going to Pay for That F***ing Wall,'" CNN, February 26, 2016, http://www.cnn.com/2016/02/26/politics/vicente-fox-donald-trump-wall-expletive.

95   Damien Cave, "Illegal Entries from Mexico Slow to Trickle," *Seattle Times*, July 5, 2011, http://www.seattletimes.com/nation-world/illegal-entries-from-mexico-slow-to-trickle.

Jennifer Agiesta, "Poll: Bush, Trump Rising Nationally for GOP, But Both Trail Clinton," CNN, July 1, 2015, http://www.cnn.com/2015/07/01/politics/donald-trump-poll-hillary-clinton-jeb-bush.

Rebecca Kaplan, "Trump: McCain Only a War Hero Because He Was Captured," CBS News, July 18, 2015, http://www.cbsnews.com/news/donald-trump-john-mccain-war-hero-captured.

96   Ben Schreckinger, "Trump Attacks McCain: 'I Like People Who Weren't Captured," *Politico*, July 18, 2015, http://www.politico.com/story/2015/07/trump-attacks-mccain-i-like-people-who-werent-captured-120317.

97   Anthony Zurcher, "Five Reasons Trump Still Tops the Polls," BBC, July 27, 2015, http://www.bbc.com/news/world-us-canada-33660969.

100   Jonathan Freedland, "The Republicans Created Donald Trump: No Wonder They Can't Stop Him," *Guardian*, March 5, 2016, http://www.theguardian.com/commentisfree/2016/mar/05/republicans-donald-trump-party-anger.

101   Nicki Rossoll, "Donald Trump Says He'll 'Get Along Fine' With Russian President Vladimir Putin," ABC News, December 20, 2015, http://abcnews.go.com/Politics/donald-trump-hell-fine-russian-president-vladimir-putin/story?id=35872623.

102   Jeremy Diamond, "Trump: World Would Be '100%' Better with Hussein, Gadhafi in Power," CNN, October 25, 2015, http://www.cnn.com/2015/10/25/politics/donald-trump-moammar-gadhafi-saddam-hussein.

103   Mark Thoma, "Is Donald Trump Right to Call NAFTA a 'Disaster'?," CBS News, October 5, 2015, http://www.cbsnews.com/news/is-donald-trump-right-to-call-nafta-a-disaster.

104   Heather Long, "Donald Trump: Tax the Rich More," CNN, August 28, 2015, http://money.cnn.com/2015/08/27/news/economy/donald-trump-economy-tax-plan.

105   Ashley Parker, "Donald Trump Says Transgender People Should Use the Bathroom They Want," *New York Times*, April 21, 2016, http://www.nytimes.com/politics/first-draft/2016/04/21/donald-trump-says-transgender-people-should-use-the-bathroom-they-want.

Maggie Haberman, "Donald Trump's More Accepting Views on Gay Issues Set Him Apart in G.O.P.," *New York Times*, April 22, 2016, http://www.nytimes.com/2016/04/23/us/politics/donald-trump-gay-rights.html.

Natalie Jackson, Evangelical Voters Don't Care that Trump's Not Religious," *Huffington Post*, January 27, 2016, http://www.huffingtonpost.com/entry/evangelical-voters-trump_us_56a8ebd9e4b0947efb661ebc.

106 Nicholas Confessore, "How the G.O.P. Elite Lost Its Voters to Donald Trump," *New York Times*, March 28, 2016, http://www.nytimes.com/2016/03/28/us/politics/donald-trump-republican-voters.html.

108 Haddon, "Donald Trump's Presidential Run."

115 "Weimar Republic Quotations," Alpha History, http://alphahistory.com/weimarrepublic/weimar-republic-quotations/#sthash.RJOD6v7C.dpuf.

   Harold Pollack, "How to Fix the Supreme Court Vacancy Mess," *Politico*, February 15, 2016, http://www.politico.com/magazine/story/2016/02/scalia-how-to-fix-supreme-court-vacancy-reform-213637#ixzz46ewhZmAo.

118 Adolf Hitler—Speech at the Berlin Sportpalast," World Future Fund, http://www.worldfuturefund.org/wffmaster/Reading/Hitler%20Speeches/Hitler%20Speech%201940.01.30.htm.

119 Tom S. Elliott, "Trump Defends Praising Putin, China's 'Strong' Response to Tiananmen Square," *National Review*, March 10, 2016, http://www.nationalreview.com/corner/432655/trump-defends-praising-putin-chinas-strong-response-tiananmen-square.

120 Patt Morrison, "Patt Morrison Asks: Robert O. Paxton Talks Fascism and Donald Trump," Los Angeles Times, March 9, 2016, http://www.latimes.com/opinion/op-ed/la-oe-patt-morrison-asks-robert-paxton-trump-fascism-20160308-story.html.

121 "Trump on Iraq: How Could We Have Been So Stupid? 'One of the Worst Decisions in the History of the Country,'" RealClearPolitics, February 17, 2016, http://www.realclearpolitics.com/video/2016/02/17/trump_on_iraq_how_could_we_have_been_so_stupid_one_of_the_worst_decisions_in_the_history_of_the_country.html.

   Lisa de Moraes, "Donald Trump Reveals Plan to Defeat ISIS: Bomb, Encircle, Send in Mobil to Take Their Oil," Deadline.com, June 16, 2015, http://deadline.com/2015/06/donald-trump-isis-bill-oreilly-jeb-bush-hillary-clinton-video-1201445840.

122 Marisa Schultz, "We Have to Beat the Savages': Trump Says More Torture Needed to Beat ISIS," *New York Post*, March 6, 2016, http://nypost.com/2016/03/06/we-have-to-beat-the-savages-trump-says-more-torture-needed-to-beat-isis.

123 Morrison, "Patt Morrison Asks."

124 Marie Solis, "This 1922 'New York Times' First-Ever Adolf Hitler Profile Is Being Compared to Trump," Mic, March 3, 2016, http://mic.com/articles/136952/this-new-york-times-first-ever-adolf-hitler-profile-1922-is-being-compared-to-trump.

125 Angela Lambert, *The Lost Life of Eva Braun* (New York: St. Martin's Press, 2007), 98.

129 Donald Trump with Tony Schwartz, *The Art of the Deal* (New York: Ballantine Books, 2004).

130 Valentina Zarya, "No One Knows What Donald Trump Did at Wharton," *Fortune*, August 14, 2015, http://fortune.com/2015/08/14/donald-trump-wharton.

Dan Spinelli, "Trump Flaunts Wharton Degree, But His College Years Remain a Mystery," *Daily Pennsylvanian*, August 19, 2015, http://www.thedp.com/article/2015/08/donald-trump-wharton-classmates.

Viser, "Even in College."

131 Viser, "Even in College."

132 Viser, "Even in College."

133 Ashley Collman, "'It Was a Very Short Evening': Candice Bergen Says She DID Go on a Date with Donald Trump in College but Only Remembers His Matching Burgundy Suit and Limo," *Daily Mail*, February 12, 2016, http://www.dailymail.co.uk/news/article-3444472/It-short-evening-Candice-Bergen-says-DID-date-Donald-Trump-college-remembers-matching-burgundy-suit-limo.html.

139 "CPI Inflation Calculator," Bureau of Labor Statistics, http://data.bls.gov/cgi-bin/cpicalc.pl?cost1=2000000&year1=1968&year2=2016.

Viser, "Even in College." https://www.bostonglobe.com/news/nation/2015/08/28/donald-trump-was-bombastic-even-wharton-business-school/3FO0j1uS5X6S8156yH3YhL/story.html. There is considerable disagreement about the amount of the loan Trump received from his father, as well as whether he was required to pay interest. On October 26, 2015, for example, CNN quoted him: "My whole life really has been a 'no' and I fought through it," Trump said in New Hampshire. "It has not been easy for me, it has not been easy for me. And you know I started off in Brooklyn, my father gave me a small loan of a million dollars." Jeremy Diamond, "Donald Trump Describes Father's 'Small Loan': $1 Million," CNN, October 27, 2015. Politifact PolitiFact wrote: "A The *National Journal* writer, S.V. Dáte, estimated figured Trump started with $40 million in 1974. That's the year he became when he became president of his father's real estate company. By one estimate, the firm was worth about $200 million and . Ddivided among Donald Trump and his four siblings, each would have received $40 million." Jon Greenberg, "Occupy Democrats Graphic Oversimplifies Trump's Inheritance," PolitiFact, December 9, 2015, http://www.politifact.com/punditfact/statements/2015/dec/09/occupy-democrats/occupy-democrats-say-simple-investment-trumps-fath/. According to BuzzFeed, Fred's largesse continued for many years: "In December 1990, a lawyer for Fred Trump walked into Trump Castle in Atlantic City and, according to reports at the time, deposited a check with the casino for $3.36 million in exchange for chips. Instead of using the chips to play in the casino, the lawyer left." Andrew Kaczynski, "Trump's Other Small Loan From Daddy-O: A Few Million Bucks to Help Pay Off His Debts," BuzzFeed, October 26, 2015, https://www.buzzfeed.

com/andrewkaczynski/you-can-rely-on-the-old-mans-money?utm_term=.
vh5z81VPL#.vi7K5VAOM.

140 Gregory Korte, "What Happened at Huntington Meadows?,"
     Cincinnati Enquirer, September 1, 2002, http://www.enquirer.com/
     editions/2002/09/01/loc_what_happened_at.html.

142 Jerome Tuccille, *Trump: The Saga of America's Most Powerful Real Estate
     Baron* (Washington, D.C.: Beard Books, 1985), 65.

143 Glenn Kessler, "Trump's Nonsensical Claim He Can Eliminate $19
     Trillion in Debt in Eight years," *Washington Post*, April 2, 2016,

144 "Donald Trump Biography."

145 Nora Caplan-Bricker, "Do Women Find Donald Trump Attractive? An
     Investigation," *Slate*, February 25, 2016, http://www.slate.com/blogs/
     xx_factor/2016/02/25/do_women_find_donald_trump_attractive_an_
     investigation.html.

146 David W. Dunlap, "1973—Meet Donald Trump," *New York Times*, July 30,
     2015, http://www.nytimes.com/times-insider/2015/07/30/1973-meet-
     donald-trump.
       Jason Parham, "The Collected Quotes of Donald Trump on 'the
     Blacks," Gawker, July 24, 2015, http://gawker.com/the-collected-quotes-
     of-donald-trump-on-the-blacks-1719961925.

148 Michael Isikoff, "Trump Challenged Over Ties to Mob-Linked Gambler
     with Ugly Past," Yahoo! News, March 7, 2016, https://www.yahoo.com/
     news/trump-challenged-over-ties-to-mob-linked-gambler-100050602.
     html.
       Report of the Division of Gaming Enforcement to the Casino
     Control Commission, "Supplemental Report on the Qualifications
     of Donald J. Trump," December 1, 1992, https://web.archive.org/
     web/20121115053737/http://www.tdbimg.com/files/2011/05/26/-trump--
     -barrett-book---supplemental-report-12-1992-6_165247103386.pdf.

149 Jonathan Mahler, "Tenants Thwarted Trump's Central Park Real Estate
     Ambitions," My AJC, April 19, 2016, http://www.myajc.com/news/news/
     tenants-thwarted-trumps-central-park-real-estate-a/nq7NM.

150 Jose Pagliery, "Donald Trump Was a Nightmare Landlord in the 1980s,"
     CNN, March 28, 2016, http://money.cnn.com/2016/03/28/news/trump-
     apartment-tenants.

151 Pagliery, "Donald Trump."

152 Pagliery, "Donald Trump."
       Donald Trump, "Big Deal: How I Do It My Way," *Vanity Fair*, August
     14, 2008, http://www.vanityfair.com/magazine/1987/12/trump_
     excerpt198712.

153 Mahler, "Tenants Thwarted Trump's."

154 Selwyn Raab, "After 15 Years in Court, Workers' Lawsuit Against Trump
     Faces Yet Another Delay," *New York Times*, June 14, 1998, http://www.

nytimes.com/1998/06/14/nyregion/after-15-years-in-court-workers-lawsuit-against-trump-faces-yet-another-delay.html.

156   David A. Graham, "The Many Scandals of Donald Trump: A Cheat Sheet," *Atlantic*, April 19, 2016, http://www.theatlantic.com/politics/archive/2016/04/donald-trump-scandals/474726.

157   Jim Geraghty, "What If Trump Doesn't Have Billions?," *National Review*, February 25, 2016, http://www.nationalreview.com/article/431915/donald-trump-worth-tax-returns-mitt-romney.

158   Janet Babin, "What It Means to Put 'Trump' on the Front of a Building," WNYC News, August 25, 2015, http://www.wnyc.org/story/what-means-put-trump-on-front-building.

159   Tom Gerencer, "Hillary Clinton Net Worth," Money Nation, April 2, 2016, http://moneynation.com/hillary-clinton-net-worth.
        Daniel Gross, "How Bernie Sanders, the Socialist, Quietly Entered the Top 4% of Earners," *Fortune*, February 28, 2016, http://fortune.com/2016/02/28/bernie-sanders-socialist-finances.

164   Gideon Resnick and Tara Wanda Merrigan, "David Duke: Trump 'Knows Who I Am,'" *Daily Beast*, February 28, 2016, http://www.thedailybeast.com/articles/2016/02/28/david-duke-i-think-trump-knows-who-i-am.html.

165   Resnick and Merrigan, "David Duke."
        Ben Schreckinger, "White Supremacist Groups See Trump Bump," *Politico*, December 10, 2015, http://www.politico.com/story/2015/12/donald-trump-white-supremacists-216620.

166   Ross Douthat, "Cracks in the Liberal Order," *New York Times*, December 26, 2015, http://www.nytimes.com/2015/12/27/opinion/sunday/cracks-in-the-liberal-order.html.

170   Marina Fang, "Donald Trump Has No Idea How to Fix Immigration, So He'll Hire People Who Do," *Huffington Post*, August 23, 2015, http://www.huffingtonpost.com/entry/donald-trump-immigration_us_55d9d16ec4b0a40aa3ab37e4.

171   Dan Lamothe and Jose A. DelReal, "Trump Backs Down from Waterboarding Comments, Says He Won't Ask Troops to Violate Law," *Washington Post*, March 4, 2016, https://www.washingtonpost.com/news/checkpoint/wp/2016/03/04/can-u-s-troops-ignore-unlawful-orders-joint-chiefs-asked-to-weigh-in-on-donald-trump.